Praise for Rob Cuesta's other books

It's not easy to describe the richness of this book, but it's never dry or technical. You'll find many gems here. How to handle objections, mental shortcuts, neuroscience driven sales process and neuro programming stuff, the role of neurotransmitters, how to turn a need into a need-want, nine stages of the sale cycle (I loved this one), importance of referrals and conversations, critical questions -you name it, and it's there, ready to be implemented. - **Lara May**

Extremely well written. Rob's advice is timely and helpful - especially for professionals who have to "sell" but don't want to appear "salesy". If you want to increase your expertise and level of comfort when promoting your services (and closing more deals), you need to read this book. - **Karol Clark**

I'm passionate about my ideas, but selling them is another thing. As I was reading this book I found myself recommending it to ALL my consultant and coaching friends. If you're a company of one... You absolutely must read this book. - **Jeff Meister**

A very good book that brought together psychology and marketing in very informative ways. I've already changed the way I engage with my clients based on the book, and am experiencing more success because of it. Definitely worth reading. - **Amazon Customer**

This is a rare guide into how people buy, with analysis of emotions, psychology and brain chemical reaction. It is rare to read a book that I, a 25 year sales pro, can apply. - **Paul Ivar**

Having read and been influenced by business and marketing gurus like Dan Kennedy, Alan Weiss, C.J. Hayden, John Jantsch, Michael Gerber, Robert Cialdini and Claude Hopkins, I still rank this as the best book I've read on how to develop my coaching business to a new level. - **JP Jakonen**

The book is well organized, easy to read, and the information is clearly presented so that it takes the guesswork out of how to create your niche and become an authority in your chosen area. I strongly recommend the book and I'm planning to use the strategies to get my work to stand out and to leave my competitors standing. - **Ernest H Johnson**

Using these techniques, my books have set me far, far apart from my competitors and even landed me all kinds of TV appearances, which put even more distance between me and my competition. - **Sandi Masori**

If you're looking for a gameplan on how to build your authority, become the recognized expert in your area, and more importantly... close more sales...then you'll definitely want to check out this book. - **Mark BM**

Great book! I made the mistake of settling down to read it after dinner. Now it is way past bed time, and my head is exploding with ideas. I'm not expecting to sleep well tonight, but tomorrow will be amazing! I'll be hitting the ground running with all the new stuff I've learned from this book. Thanks! Rob doesn't take the motivational "You can do it if you believe you can" angle. The book is full of practical advice, real-life scenarios and examples, and tips you can take immediate action on. - **Christine F. Abela**

FUNNEL HACKS FOR AUTHORS

Vol. 1

FUNNEL HACKS FOR AUTHORS

VOLUME 1: Turn Your Book into a List-Building, Money-Making, Client-Getting Machine

Rob Cuesta

Brightflame Books

TORONTO, CANADA

Funnel Hacks for Authors

© 2018 Rob Cuesta

Published by BrightFlame Books, Burlington, Ontario

Could a book help you grow your business?
Download our free business growth guide
www.BrightFlameBooks/16ways

Contents

PART FOUR
Setting Up Your Free + Shipping Funnel

STOP! BEFORE YOU GO ANY FURTHER

Register your copy of this book right now to get instant access to the following bonuses as a thank you for being a reader:

- Clickable import links for all the funnels and email automations in this book.
- Editable files of all the sample emails so you can tailor them to your business and/or import them into any email software you want.
- A PDF edition of this book that you can print out and make notes on.
- Free updates to future editions of the book.

Visit www.BrightFlameBooks.com/FunnelBonus

We know that some of the images in this book are small, and they may be hard to read in print or on your e-reader. To make life simpler, the bonuses for this book include a full-resolution PDF of the complete book. You'll be able to zoom in and view the images up close.

A NOTE ON SCREENSHOTS

Shortly after we completed the manuscript of this book, both ActiveCampaign and ClickFunnels updated their user interface. It's one of the joys of writing "how to" technical books: just when you think you're done, someone shifts the goalposts.

Fortunately, the changes—at least as they concern what we're doing in this book—were primarily cosmetic. In Active-Campaign, the main menu has moved from the top menu bar to a sidebar down the left of the screen. In ClickFunnels, they've added an initial dashboard page. Neither change is major, and you'll still be able to follow along easily.

We're working on an updated version of the book with new screenshots. In the meantime, however, you can still follow the instructions in this book—just be aware that some options may be in slightly different places on the screen.

And remember: if you register your copy of the book, **we'll send you an updated version of the book free when it's ready.**

Register at www.BrightFlameBooks.com/FunnelBonus

Preface

I've been teaching professionals to write a book as the core of their personal brand since 2010.

It all started when I was giving a seminar on marketing for coaches, speakers and consultants. We'd just broken for lunch on the second day, and one of the participants came up to talk to me. "Great workshop," she said. "I've learnt so much. You really should write a book. After all" — and this is the bit that really got to me — "*that's what experts do.*"

That's what experts do: they write books.

Within three months, I'd written my first book, *More Clients, More Money, More Fun,* and I was teaching my clients to do it too.

In fact, I believe writing a book is so critical for anyone who makes their living by charging for their knowledge, experience or expertise that, in 2014, I focused the business entirely on books as marketing tools. Today, my team and I at BrightFlame Books help dozens of professionals every year to position themselves as leaders in their industry by writing and publishing a signature book, and launching it to bestseller status.

Of course, these days, there are a lot of people teaching you that you need to write a book. There are also lots of ghostwriters out there — some better than others. The big gap, however, is what comes next. It's one thing to have a book. It's another to know what to do with it.

This book began as two sessions of a program called the Author-Experts Insiders Circle which teaches professionals like you how to use a book as a tool for business growth. Each month, I share a strategy or a full-blown marketing campaign for the program members to implement—for example setting up your email follow-up sequences—and once a quarter we have a full-day session (I call them our Get S*** Done Days) where we go through something more in-depth or complicated—for example, setting up your core marketing funnels.

Visit <u>www.HowExpertsGetClients.com for more details.</u>

A note on affiliate links

I deliberately built this book around two specific tools: ActiveCampaign for email marketing and ClickFunnels for funnel creation. If you don't already use these two tools, you'll find links in this book to pages where you can sign up for accounts with both of those companies. Those links are affiliate links, which means that if you sign up using those links, I get a small percentage of what you pay as a reward from the company.

However, the reason I chose those tools is not because of the commission. The reason I recommend these tools is that they are the tools I use in my own business.

A few years ago, I needed to change my email marketing platform. For various reasons, I'd ended up with two systems: part of my list was on one of the low-end email platforms which was costing me $49/month, but the bulk of my list was on a higher-end platform for which I was paying $397/month. Neither platform was giving me what I needed, so I decided it was time to switch.

I went through an exercise to compare all the major email platforms, right from free/$20-a-month systems all the way up to systems that cost a $200-$400 a month even at the starter level. I was looking for something that was powerful, scalable, easy to use, and wouldn't break the bank.

ActiveCampaign was the clear winner. So, I switched my own lists across, and I started to tell my clients to use it.

The main reason I recommend ActiveCampaign is that when you're first starting out it's simple and cheap. I have some clients who, by their own admission, are "technically challenged" but can handle themselves very well in ActiveCampaign: I'm not sure they would cope as well with any of the more complex systems.

As your list grows, however, and your needs become more sophisticated, ActiveCampaign can keep up with that evolution, and that's the key reason for using it. You can make your follow up as simple or as complex as you want/need.

If you're using a different system, you could skip the technical sections about ActiveCampaign and simply implement the campaigns I describe in the system you're used to (or you can take my advice and switch to ActiveCampaign).

However, even if you use another system, I recommend that you read through those technical sections because you'll see just how powerful it is.

The other major reason I recommend ActiveCampaign is because it integrates very easily with ClickFunnels: all it takes is a couple of clicks and a copy/paste when you first set up your system. From that point on, it's just a couple of clicks to add people to your lists from ClickFunnels.

And if you do decide to use ActiveCampaign, you'll find links in this book to load all the email sequences directly into your system automatically. If you use a different platform, you'll have to copy and paste the emails in by hand (and I'll give you links so you can download them).

Similarly, if you use ClickFunnels, I'll give you links so that you can import the funnels straight into your account and all you have to do is change the text and images. If you use a different funnel building tool, then you're going to have to create the funnels from scratch.

Both ActiveCampaign and ClickFunnels have free 14-day trials, so you could follow the instructions in this book, see how you get on with the software, and start getting new readers, all without paying out a single cent.

TRY ACTIVECAMPAIGN FOR FREE

If you'd like to give ActiveCampaign a spin, you can try it free for two weeks by creating a trial account.

Visit http://bit.ly/ACrobcs

A note on Actionetics/ClickFunnels

By writing this book, I've probably earned the hatred of a lot of die-hard ClickFunnels users and consultants because I didn't recommend ClickFunnels' own email system, Actionetics.

I have nothing against Actionetics. Indeed, if you don't want to use ActiveCampaign—and especially if you already have a large list, or you believe you can grow your list quickly—Actionetics would be my runner-up recommendation, simply because it's already integrated with the main ClickFunnels software.

So, why didn't I go straight to Actionetics?

First, I don't use it myself, so promoting it would go against my rule of only recommending the tools that I actually use in my own business. And because I don't use it, it would be difficult for me to show you what to do, and I wanted this book to be a "follow-along" manual that you can sit with and implement as you read.

Second, Actionetics requires a $297 subscription to ClickFunnels right from the start. That's fine if you have an established business with a big mailing list, but if you're just starting out, or if your list is smaller simply because you're in a business that doesn't need a list of tens of thousands, that level of investment is hard to justify.

So, even though I'd make more money from commissions by recommending Actionetics, I'll stick to the system I know, and what I believe is—for many readers of this book—in your best interest.

You can get started with the tools in this book for as little as $28 a month, and your payments will only go up as your business grows.

Introduction

In this book, you'll build two funnels that I believe every non-fiction author should have to get you readers and turn your readers into clients.

Ultimately, this book is about connecting with our readers more efficiently and effectively. When we're using a book to grow our business, we need to connect with our readers, because those are our potential clients.

Now, we could do that one on one—when somebody buys our book, we could send them a nice personalized letter, or we could attach it to a carrier pigeon and have it fly to them and deliver it personally—but that's not particularly efficient, and it's probably not that effective.

Instead, we need to automate our connection process as much as possible, and we're going to use ClickFunnels and ActiveCampaign to do it, for reasons that I explained in the Preface.

As you read the book, you'll be building the funnels and email sequences.

If you're using different platforms, you'll be able to follow along with the principles but you're going to have to build the funnels and sequences from scratch.

A major objective for me as I wrote this book was to make it as simple as possible for you to implement.

A lot of the content for this book is pre-built: I will give you funnels that you can import directly into your ClickFunnels account and email sequences that you can import directly into your ActiveCampaign account. As much as possible, all you'll have to do is to customize and adapt the templates I give you and update them with your own content rather than recreating from scratch.

The idea is not to turn you into a ClickFunnels or Active-Campaign consultant. Rather, I will teach you what you need to know to set up and manage the core funnels with ActiveCampaign and ClickFunnels as a business owner. It's not about being able to sit down and create absolutely any funnel you want—although you'll have all the skills that you need by the time you've been through this book.

It's also not a "how to automate all your marketing" book, a "how to do email marketing" book, or a copywriting book: instead, at the end of the book I'll share some resources to help you with all of those.

The first part of the book is quite theoretical: what funnels are, why you need them, what they look like, and so on. It sets the context for everything we will be doing.

In the second and subsequent parts, however, we get down into the nuts and bolts of implementation.

My promise to you, however, is that by the time you've finished reading this book and implementing what I've taught you, you will have your first three sales funnels online, you will have connected them to your autoresponder, and you'll be able to start driving leads into them, following up with those leads, and generating sales.

I will take you as far as I can without actually doing it for you. From there on, how quickly you get your funnels up and running and start driving traffic to them is up to you.

Who this is not for

If you've already got a massive list, and you're selling to it and they're buying, then you probably have a lot of this in place anyway, so this book is not for you.

It's also not for you if you don't want to learn any technology skills at all. If you just want somebody to take this away from you and do it, then you are probably better off hiring a consultant. But, if you want to be able to at least brief a consultant on what you need them to do, and understand the work they're doing so that you know what's possible and what isn't, what's involved and what's reasonable in terms of fees, then this is a great book for you.

It's also not for you if you couldn't care less about connecting with your readers or you don't want to build your profile, your personal brand, or your credibility. If all you want to do is set up a funnel and drive people to anything they will buy simply as a way of making money — and you don't care whether it's the right product or service for them or whether it's the right product or service for your business to be promoting in the first place — then this book is not for you either.

And with that out of the way, let's dive into why you need funnels in your business.

PART ONE

An Introduction to Funnels

1

Why Funnels?

At some point, every nonfiction author thinks to themselves at least one of the following:

- "I've written this book, but no one is buying it."
- "My book is selling, but I've got no idea who bought it."
- "I've given away all these copies of my book because my coach told me to, but I can't get people to take the next step."

I chose the funnels in this book specifically to address those three problems.

Ultimately, it's all a matter of connecting with your readers.

It's about getting people to sign up and give you their contact details so that you can start or continue a conversation.

It's about getting someone who bought your book on Amazon, Barnes and Noble, a bookstore, or anywhere else — places that don't tell you who their customers are, so you have no way of finding out who bought your book — to hold up their hands and tell you.

And if you give away your books, it's about getting the people you give them to to reach out and tell you that they're ready for the next step and that they want to do something else with you.

There are also many events that you can participate in as an author — giveaways, conferences, virtual summits, panels, etc. — and funnels are a great way to use those opportunities to grow your audience. All you have to do is tell the participants in the event that you have a free resource for them and send them to your funnel.

In the longer term, of course, simply connecting with readers isn't enough. You need to build a community or *tribe*. The problem is, that can be a full-time job in its own right. The funnels are designed to automate the process of building your tribe and engaging them as much as possible and make it easier.

A lot of people say "I already have a website that I paid money for. Why can't I just use that? Why do I need to build a funnel separately?"

The problem is that your website is simply too distracting.

Nowadays, pretty much the only way to get people to your website is to pay for them to go there. So, you're running pay-per-click ads on Google, Facebook, Instagram, LinkedIn, or wherever to get people to your website, and when they get there you have no idea what they're doing. There's no plan of what they're going to do on your website because it's not designed to get them to take action.

So, when somebody comes to your home page they start reading about you. Then they see a menu at the top of the page, they click on the "About Me" link and they start reading your profile.

But then, on the sidebar of your About Me page there's a list of your latest blog posts and they spot what looks like an interesting post. So now they don't finish reading your profile either, and they're off reading your blog and disappearing down a rabbit hole.

Worse yet, Facebook flashes up that there's a message for them, and suddenly they're leaving your website altogether — and remember: you PAID for them to come there.

Most websites are little more than a glorified brochure. They're all about how wonderful you are and how wonderful your services are. But there's nothing that prompts people to take the next step.

Websites are also incredibly confusing. And if there's one thing you'll learn in business it's that a confused mind never buys.

I remember reading about a study that was carried out in supermarkets in the UK a few years ago. Now, baked beans are big business in the UK, and there are hundreds of choices available to consumers: different brands, different sizes of can, single cans versus multi-packs, beans with or without sausages, low sugar, low salt… the choice is endless.

One of the major chains stacked a shelf in one of their branches with just 20 different varieties of baked beans — a fraction of the total product range — and set up cameras to see what people did: What were they buying? How were they buying? How much were they spending?

The results were shocking. A small number would just walk up and buy the brand they always bought, completely ignoring everything else. The rest would spend time looking at the range, they would pick up a can, put it back, pick up another, put it back, compare labels, and compare prices, but *a large proportion of shoppers would simply walk away without buying anything.*

So then, the supermarket cleared the shelf and restocked it with just six different varieties. Again, they set up cameras and watched. Again, there were a few people who simply walked up, picked up their usual brand, and walked away. But for the rest, they would walk up, scan the shelf, make a quick choice, and walk away with beans in their shopping basket.

Cutting the range of choices *increased* sales of beans overall. Why? Because when there were twenty choices, consumers simply couldn't choose. They were worried they would make the wrong choice. That the brand they picked might not be as good as another, that they might not like the taste, or whatever.

But when there were only six to choose from, people were much happier to pick one. Maybe in their mind they thought they had a one-in-six chance of making a good choice (compared to only one in twenty in the other experiment).

The main point is this: giving people fewer options results in better response.

And a funnel starts with a single option.

The idea of a funnel is that you take people to a page that basically says, "Give me your contact details and you'll get something in exchange." So they have to decide whether it's worth giving you their details in order to get that, and if they decide that it isn't, there's nothing else for them to do. They can't click on an About Me page. They can't start exploring your blog. They can't browse your testimonials. They can't do anything on your site because they haven't got there yet.

Now, some people say, "but what if they don't want it and they leave?"

Let them.

If they don't want your free or low-cost information, what chance is there that they'll pay for your premium products and services?

But if they do decide to take that first step, what next?

That's the subject of our next chapter, The Client Journey.

2

The Client Journey

Once someone is in your funnel—once they opt in—you can take them to your home page and they can explore to their heart's content. Once they've taken that first step of handing over their contact details—and perhaps even paying for something—they've embarked on what I call The Client Journey.

The Client Journey is a model I set out in my book *Just Sign Here!* It describes how we take someone who's never heard of us and turn them, step-by-step, into a buyer, a repeat buyer, and then ultimately a referrer.

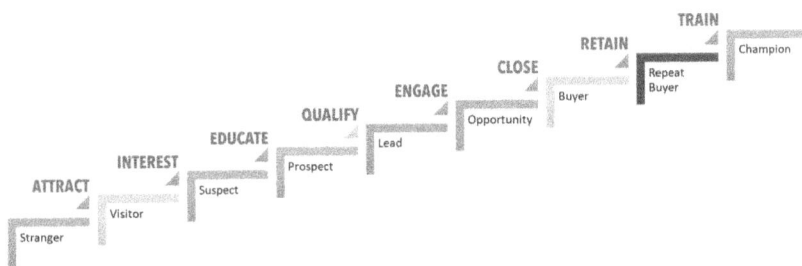

I like to explain using the metaphor of a seaside gift store.

Every day, hundreds of people walk past the gift store who have never heard of it before — we call them **Strangers**.

Now, people walking past aren't going to buy. We need them to at the very least step inside the door — to *attract* them enough that they become what we call a **Visitor**.

So, as a store owner, your first thought should be "How do I get people to notice my store and walk in?" For a website, the equivalent is "How do I get all those people who are out there on the Internet to come to my website?"

To do that, our gift store owner might put up a poster or an A-board with an eye-catching message ("Free ice-cream with every purchase today!") or stand an assistant on the sidewalk giving passers by a sample of something.

Of course, simply looking into a shop doesn't make someone want to buy. We need to *Interest* them in the products available and get them to engage so that we can identify the **Suspects** — people who we think might buy eventually, even if we haven't yet confirmed their total level of interest.

Our gift shop owner will want visitors to step into the shop, browse the shelves, and pick up and compare some of the items. To do that, they will put attractive gifts on display where they can be easily seen. They might mark them out with signs and special displays so that shoppers will want to pick them up.

Online, you'll use images of your free report or other gifts to get people to give you their contact details.

If they do that, then they are telling us that they want to know more. So, this is where we lay the groundwork for the next step: we *Educate* them. In this step, we want them to start to identify specific products or services that match their need — at which point they become a **Prospect** — or decide that, in fact, we are not a good match for them.

In your business, you might offer case studies, special reports, white papers, free video training, and other resources that educate them about their problem. You may need to show them that they have a problem they didn't realize. Or perhaps they know they have the problem but they don't realize there's a solution.

In our gift store, the owner might put labels on the shelves that tell the shopper about the product: "This scarf is made from the hair of 500 alpacas bred in the foothills of the Andes. Each spring, the villagers of Chucama go into the mountains to shear their herds, then the hair is carried down mountain paths on the backs of goats to the town of..." and so on.

Having established that the Prospect is potentially interested, this is the point at which we can start to ask questions so that we can *Qualify* them and establish whether they're an actual **Lead**.

So, in our imaginary gift shop, what happens? A member of staff will walk up and start asking them questions. "I noticed you were looking at the alpaca scarves... is that what you came in for today? Who's the gift for? What's your budget? What kind of things do you enjoy or what kind of things does the person you're going to give it to enjoy?"

In your own business, you're going to find out about their situation and the problem they're facing, so that you can determine whether your products are suitable for them. Because if they're not, you can send them away. And if they are, then you can start to talk to them about options and *Engage* them — keep up a conversation with them — until they settle on the option they want, at which point you have identified an **Opportunity** and we can *Close* them into a **Buyer**.

After that you're going to give them a good enough experience that you can *Retain* them so they will come back and be a **Repeat Buyer**.

And finally, you're going to *Train* them in how to make referrals so that they become our **Champions**.

That's the model, and our objective with anybody who comes to us is to figure out where they are on that model.

Are they a Stranger who knows nothing about us? In that case, we have to interest them and educate them.

Or are they somebody who has been in our community for a while? If so, they're probably a good prospect and we just have to qualify them, engage them, and close them.

Many business owners make the mistake of not figuring out where someone is on that journey. And, usually, they assume people are much further along the journey than they actually are, so they go straight for the close.

At every stage of the journey, our objective is simply to figure out how to get the person to the next stage. If someone is a Stranger, how do I attract them to my website? If someone is a Prospect, what I do have to do to qualify them and turn them into a lead?

I'm not going to take a Prospect and try to sell to them without knowing whether the solutions I have are even right for them. I have to qualify them first, and then I'm going to have to engage them with the specific options and close them.

How does any of this relate to funnels?

A funnel is simply a way of moving a buyer further along the client journey.

Often, we can use a single funnel to move people through several steps, with each element of the funnel — a page, an email sequence, etc. — designed to move them forwards by a single step.

For example, you might have a funnel that starts with an opt-in box so the visitor can request a free report. Then, on the thank you page, you show them a video that educates them immediately and at the end you invite them to click through to a quiz or assessment which is actually designed to qualify them. In that funnel, you've taken a Visitor all the way to Lead.

Now, the Visitor might complete that funnel in a single visit, but what if they don't? That's where follow up becomes essential. If someone opted in but didn't watch the video, we can send them emails to invite them to watch the video. If they don't take the quiz, we can send them emails to encourage them to take it.

For every funnel you create, you need to be clear on where someone should be on the Client Journey as they enter the funnel, and where they are going to end up at the end of it. And for the funnels you'll see later in this book, I've done that work for you: I'll tell you which stage it is suitable for, and which stage it's designed to take people to next.

The Core Funnels

In this book, I am going to show you two of the core funnels every expert-author needs to have in place in order to turn strangers at least into buyers.

The specific funnels you're going to build are

1) The Reader Bonus funnel
2) The Free Plus Shipping funnel

The **Reader Bonus** funnel is designed to get someone who has read your book to hold up their hand, metaphorically, and tell you that they are ready for more and they want to take the next step.

The **Free Plus Shipping** funnel is a great way to get leads and turn them almost immediately into buyers.

In future books, I'll show you how to build the other three core funnels:

3) The **Street Team** funnel
4) The **Ticking Timebomb** funnel
5) The **Evergreen Webinar** funnel

3

The Value Ladder

Underpinning everything we're discussing in this book is a model based on what Russell Brunson, the creator of ClickFunnels, calls the Value Ladder. It coincides very nicely with a concept that I introduced in my book *Premium!* so I use slightly modified language that more closely matches the language in that book.

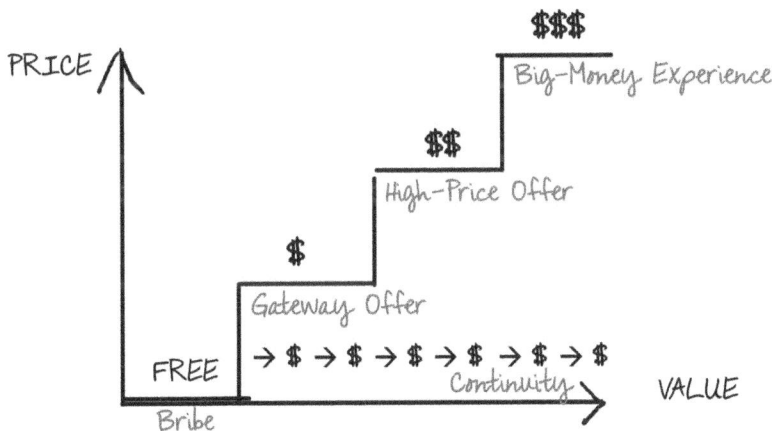

PRICE

$$$
Big-Money Experience

$$
High-Price Offer

$
Gateway Offer

FREE
→ $ → $ → $ → $ → $ → $
Continuity

Bribe

VALUE

The idea is simply that we can't go straight to high price, high value sales: we have to help people to get there. To do that, we create a ladder that takes people from a point where they've never paid us anything, to where they're paying us a high fee, in exchange for which we are delivering huge amounts of value.

Our objective is to stay on the ladder: so, we deliver some value for free. Then we deliver some more value but charge for it. Then we ramp up the value some more, and increase our fees accordingly.

What we can't afford to do in business is to stray too far from the ladder. I've seen too many businesses that tried to deliver tremendous value without charging for it — effectively pushing themselves into the bottom right corner — and they went bust because they couldn't make a profit. Delivering massive value usually requires us to be participating a lot. Often, it means working with people individually or in very small groups, creating great experiences, and delivering resources. If your price is too low, you can't afford to maintain that level of value creation and delivery.

At the same time, we've all seen businesses up in the top left corner, charging high fees but not delivering real value. They may survive for a short period of time, but eventually the news spreads and people stop buying from them — thank goodness! If you try to charge a high price for very low value, you'll get a terrible brand, and people start asking for refunds and telling all their friends that you're a scammer.

So, you have to stay on, or close to, the ladder.

Climbing the ladder

We start the ladder with a free offer, which I refer to as the **Bribe** because it's what you use to bribe visitors to give you their contact details.

Then you take them up to a relatively low-priced offer which I call the **Gateway Offer**. And the reason I call it a Gateway Offer is because it's a way of getting someone to cross the threshold and become a buyer.

From there, they are ready to move up to your **High-Price Offer**, and finally up to your **Big Money Experiences**.

Along the way, there's a second option from free, which is to put them into a **Continuity Program**, where they pay a small monthly subscription fee over and over again. It means that, although they're paying us a low amount each month, over time it adds up to a large amount for us.

Let's look at each of these in detail.

Bribes

Bribes, as I said, are something that you offer for free to get someone's contact details.

Typical bribes are:

- Book
- Ebook
- Report
- Quiz/Assessment

- Video (or DVD)
- MP3 (or CD)
- Webinar
- Worksheets
- Infographics
- Checklists
- Free challenge

They can be free or they can be "free" in quotes: what that means is that you can actually get someone to pay for a free product. How? The Free Plus Shipping offer: you give them the product at no cost, but you ask them to pay a small amount for delivery.

Now, the smart thing that your customers don't realize is that the shipping cost is set to cover the raw cost of the product too, as we'll see later.

Gateway Offers

Of course, none of this happens until someone who has never heard of you comes to your place of business, and the way you're going to get people to your website is typically by paying for traffic, for example through pay-per-click ads. If you're in a bricks-and-mortar business, you might be paying for traffic by advertising in the local paper or directories or by running radio ads.

However you get someone to your business, the best way to get people to visit is usually to pay for them to be sent to you.

And we set up Gateway Offers because that's how we pay for that traffic: the Gateway offer is what gets us to break-even. Indeed, even though people are paying for the Gateway Offer, we may not be making any money from it: our objective can be simply to get the buyer to pay what it's cost us to get them this far. Once we achieve that, however, anything they buy from that point onwards is pure profit, because **once somebody has bought your gateway offer you don't have to pay to market to them anymore**. They're inside your community. They're committed. They're going to be engaging with you because they've paid you money. So, the cost of marketing to them goes away.

Gateway offers are typically going to be around $20-$1,000, and often they're going to be at the lower end of that. But this is how we get someone to show us that they're interested, and in particular that they're interested enough to pay.

Typical gateway offers include:

- Seminar/Workshop
- DVD
- Info-product
- Paid webinar
- Paid challenge
- Short program ("Book study")

These are all "show me how" products: you're not promising to hold their hand as they do it; you're not promising to work through it with them; in fact, you're not promising any personal support at all.

The client is buying the rights to attend a workshop, or to watch a video or a webinar, or whatever, but they're not necessarily going to interact personally with you or with anyone on your team.

The main thing is that we want our gateway offer to be an impulse buy. Now, if your gateway offer costs $20 that's simple. But if it's $97, or even $997 (because you're aiming at a

$3,000 high-price offer) then it's harder to get someone to pay that for their first ever purchase.

That's when you should use the "Free Plus Shipping" offer as a "free" bribe: if you can get someone to pay $7.95 for a free product, it leads them more naturally into a $97 or $500 gateway offer.

High-Price Offers

High price offers are typically priced $1,000-$10,000.

At this level, you're primarily selling accountability and support: it's often referred to as "done with you" (as opposed to "done for you" which we will discuss in the next section). In other words, you are showing your clients how to do something, and then watching them as they do it and providing live feedback in the moment.

Typical High-Price Offers are:

- Large-group event (e.g. 3-day workshop)
- Training program (e.g. 90-Day Bootcamp)
- Info-product with support
- Group coaching
- Laser coaching

At this level, you might hire a coach or a team of specialists to work with your clients and provide support (so that you can reserve direct one-on-one access to you for your Big Money Experiences).

Big Money Experiences

Our final aim is to get clients into what I call Big Money Experiences. As you'd expect, the defining feature of these is price—and by extension, value. Typically, the fee for a Big Money Experience is going to be $5,000 and up—the exact amount will depend on the industry you are in.

Now, notice that there's an overlap with the high-price offers ($1,000-$10,000). Obviously, if your high-price offer is $1,000, your big money experience is likely to be closer to the $5,000 price point, and if your high-price offer is $10,000, your big money experience is going to be much higher—more like $30,000, $50,000, maybe even $100,000 or more.

I always advise my clients to reserve their intensive one-on-one support for clients at this level: try to avoid working with clients individually if they are paying you less than this.

In some industries that might seem difficult to achieve, but you can get very creative. Imagine you're a chiropractor. It's easy to assume that a chiropractor has to work one-on-one. And yet, there's a chiropractor down the road from me who has four treatment rooms running simultaneously all day long. She has a client in each room, and she'll make an adjustment then ask them to rest and be aware of their body. Then she moves to the next room and does the same with the next client. Eventually, she circles round to the first client again and makes the next adjustment.

Of course, if someone wants individual attention, it's available... but it costs more.

Not only that, but rather than sell single sessions, the way many health practitioners do, she signs patients up to multi-session packages that cost anything from $800-$2,000. The result? With all four treatment rooms full, she's typically working on $5,000-worth of clients at any one time.

You can take the same model even further. I remember reading about a hand surgery clinic in—I believe—Cleveland, OH. In the clinic, the operating theater is set up with multiple operating tables arranged in a star around the surgeon who stands in the middle. The surgeon moves from table to table, carrying out the next stage of the operation at each one then leaving a team at each table to carry out intermediate steps until he makes his way back round the ring to them.

So, even in situations where you might think you have to work one-on-one with people, you can still find ways to be leveraged.

And if you have to sell your time hour by hour, you have the option of selling packages of time instead, and getting your clients to commit to a serious fee in order to have one-on-one access to you.

One of my clients, Vanessa, worked for many years selling coaching hour-by-hour for about $200. One of the first changes we made when she started working with me was to get her selling packages of time instead of single hours, and to raise her fees.

We also switched her target market, so that instead of working with individuals she started targeting organizations where she could work with multiple executives at the same time.

The result? The average value of a client went from $800 to $8,000 in a short space of time

So, ask yourself: what would it mean to you to add an extra zero to your income?

Of course, when you're charging "big money" it means you have to offer "big value" in return. It's not a case of simply taking something that you used to charge $500 for and changing the price overnight to $5,000 (although I have met some clients who could do that, simply because they were seriously undercharging!)

Instead, you have to ask yourself, "If I'm going to charge $5,000, how do I create more than $5,000 of value? What other components can I add to this product or program to ramp up the value delivery?"

Typical offers at this price point include

- Done-for-you services
- Mastermind groups
- VIP/Power Days
- Small-group Events and Retreats
- Personal coaching or mentoring

As an example, I could take the contents of this book and turn it into a $5,000-$10,000 experience quite simply.

As you work through the book, you're going to have to write copy for the pages, write your own versions of the emails, and create graphics for your books and your products and services.

But imagine that instead I invited you to a two-day in-person workshop, and I had a team of copywriters, graphic designers, and web designers there, at the back of the room, so that over the course of the two days you told them what you wanted and they created it for you, and by the end of the event everything was set up without you having to do any of the technical or creative work.

See? I've taken a $20 book and turned it into a $10,000 event just by changing how it's delivered.

Planning the Value Ladder

As you build your value ladder, start with the end in mind. The mistake a lot of experts make is they start by thinking about their free offer, because that's the easiest thing to do.

So, they write your free report or your book or whatever, and then suddenly they're scrabbling around thinking "what am I going to do next? Let's do a workshop. Great!"

They get them in the workshop and suddenly they're thinking "Oh heck what am I going to sell them next?"

They have no idea where the client is going to end up, or at what price point.

It makes much more sense to figure out your big money experience and its price first, and to work back from there.

In fact, the way I built my marketing business was that I figured out the big money experience, then I figured out the Gateway Offer to lead straight into it: I skipped the high-price offer altogether!

Back in 2011, when I started running business growth programs and workshops for professional advisers, the big money experience was an $18,000 done-for-you program. The way I got people into it was through a gateway workshop which was either $147 or $497 for a VIP upgrade. There was nothing in between.

In fact, there was nothing in between for quite a while until, eventually, I started backfilling the value ladder with programs and products that were pitched in the middle. For several years, however, the program was running with the high-end Big Money Experience and the low-end Gateway, and it worked very well.

So, it's possible to build those two points and be making good money, then fill in the middle. And it's much better than starting with just the low end in place and trying to figure out how to make a living while you build the top end!

EXERCISE

OK, it's time for a quick exercise.

1) Decide what your Big Money Experience is going to be, and what you'll charge for it.

Then, work back down the value ladder and plan how you're going to get people into that Big Money Experience:

2) What will your High-Price Offer be? And what will you charge for it?

3) What will your Gateway Offer be? And what will you charge for it?

4) What will you offer as a Bribe? Will it be free or "free"? (Hint: you'll be creating a free plus shipping offer in this book!)

Continuity Income

A question for you: would you rather have 7 people paying you $1,000 a month, or 1,000 people paying you $7 a month?

Let me make it easier: imagine that in each scenario six of those people decide to cancel. Now which do you prefer?

There is a lot to be said from the stability and security you feel when you have a continuity program up and running.

Typically, in a continuity program, people are going to be paying $7-$97 a month. You'll also hear the term *micro-continuity*, which refers specifically to continuity programs where the subscription is low (under $20/month)

The reason I say the upper limit is $100 is that anything above that is starting to turn into a high-priced offer that looks more like a long-term group coaching program.

In reality, Continuity programs are about getting people to pay you to be your lead and to keep them engaged. The kind of offers that fall into this category include:

- Software as a Service
- Paid newsletter
- Monthly club
- Regular livecasts

Software as a service is great if you can turn part of what you do into some form of software or app. If you can make it so that the only way they can keep getting the result they want is by using the software, then you've created a customer for life.

In fact, you can think of ClickFunnels as a continuity pro-gram: people are paying $97-$297 a month, and some of them just need the funnels and that's all they'll ever buy, but a very large proportion of those people go on to buy Russell Brunson's products and coaching programs and everything else. Along the way, he is engaging them every month through his books, workshops, and livestreams that he runs for free for ClickFunnels subscribers. It's a very clever business model, because basically his leads are paying hundreds of dollars every month to stay in his list.

Now, you may be surprised to see **Paid Newsletters** on this list. So often, we see companies offering us their free newsletter, and what it really means is they want permission to pester the hell out of you month after month until you finally have enough and unsubscribe.

So how do we get people to pay for a newsletter? Well part of it is down to the value that we're creating, and part of it is that while people may not pay for an online newsletter, they will pay for exactly the same content if you print it and mail it to them. And there are fulfillment companies out there that will do that for you for a very low cost.

Better yet, if you've got a printed newsletter, you can get other businesses to pay you to advertise in it. That's almost impossible with an online newsletter, especially a free online newsletter.

It's also much easier to justify to yourself running pay-per-click ads to send people to subscribe to a paid newsletter than it is to send them to opt in for your free newsletter.

Finally, if someone is paying for a newsletter, they are much more likely to buy something else.

In fact, That's the big thing about all of these continuity programs: if someone is paying you even $7 a month, they're far more likely to then buy something else from you than someone who is just reading your emails.

Monthly Clubs are very similar in operation to paid newsletters in that someone is paying to get content from you every month. All that changes is the medium.

A great is example is "book (or video or product) of the month"-type clubs where you send new content each month. You can do this for almost any type of product. There's a company called Wen haircare, for example, that has turned shampoo into a continuity program: every month they send you a box of haircare products. There are similar companies for socks, ties, razors and many other products.

Even Amazon has got in on the game: it offers Subscribe and Save on many of its smaller products. Why? Because if you're buying a low-cost product and it's consumable (like a face cream or a diet supplement), they know you'll probably need it again. And they don't want you to buy next month's supply from someone else, so they offer you a small discount to let them ship it to you automatically.

Finally, there's **Regular Livecasts**. This is the other side of Russell Brunson's business model. Alongside the ClickFunnels software as a service he is constantly interacting with his customers: weekly webinars, ad hoc Facebook Live broadcasts, and even entire one-day and multi-day workshops that he broadcasts online — all designed to keep ClickFunnels users engaged and inside his community.

So, part of your subscription — whatever model you choose — can be regular live casts.

The key to all of these formats is *leverage*. None of the models has any kind of regular personal one-on-one contact. The one piece of personal interaction that I always tell my clients to include is this: when someone joins your continuity program, offer them a short conversation with you one-on-one. The reason this is so important is that first, they connect to you as a real person, which makes it harder for them to cancel. Second, whether they've just paid you $7, $20, $97 or whatever, they are an incredibly valuable lead because they are already **a buyer**. So, that first conversation with them is a sales call to see whether you can move them into the gateway offer, the high priced offer. or the big-money experience.

Exercise

OK, it's time for another quick exercise.

1) Do you have a continuity program already?

2) If not, what could you offer as a continuity or micro-continuity program?

3) What price point would you set?

PART TWO

Email Automation with ActiveCampaign

4

Introducing ActiveCampaign

Before we get into the detail of the funnels, it's time to introduce email marketing and my recommended email platform, ActiveCampaign.

In this book, we will set up two lists—collections of people's names and email addresses—that you need for your funnels, and the email follow-up sequences that will be sent to those people.

I'll also be introducing you to the fundamentals of email marketing, and although I'm basing the content of this book on ActiveCampaign, you should be able to follow along and translate what I'm teaching you into whatever email system you use.

Specifically, we are going to set up lists for people who purchase your Free Plus Shipping offer and for people who request your reader bonuses.

We'll also be creating a special follow-up sequence—what Ryan Deiss calls your *Indoctrination Sequence*—which people only get sent the very first time they sign up to receive information from you.

As I said at the start of this book, the idea is to make things as simple as possible for you. So, if you're using ActiveCampaign you'll be able to install the framework of the follow-up sequences directly into your system. If you're not, you'll need to set things up manually.

STOP! BEFORE YOU GO ANY FURTHER!

If you don't have an ActiveCampaign account and you want to follow along, you'll need to sign up.

You can get a 14-day trial (long enough to work through the exercises in this book) by visiting

http://bit.ly/ACrobcs

5

Dashboard and Lists

Once you've signed up, the first screen you'll be taken to is the Dashboard. If this is a new account, you won't see much in there:

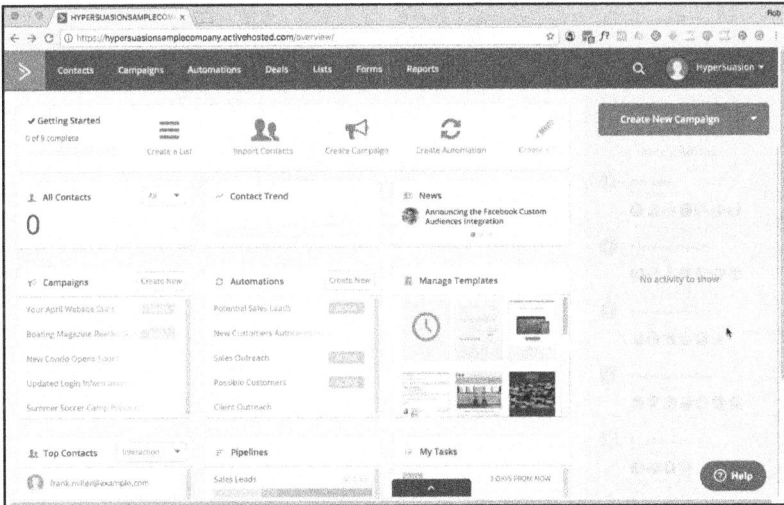

Up at the top, there is a Getting Started checklist, and by the time you finish this book, you'll have completed most of the items on it.

Once you've set up some lists and you have automations running and contacts signing up, you'll be able to see what's going on in your system in the timeline that runs down the right-hand side of the screen. You'll see who's subscribed or unsubscribed, how many people have opened an email, who is clicking links in your emails, and more.

Below the checklist is a panel that shows you how many contacts you have—you can switch between the total count (which is what your monthly fee is based on) and active contacts (i.e. who haven't unsubscribed).

One of the things I love about ActiveCampaign compared to other email systems is that you only pay once for someone, even if they're on multiple lists. In the past, I used a different email provider and I was quite surprised when my payment went up one month, because my list hadn't grown very much. What had happened, however, was that people were signing up for three or four different lists and they were being counted multiple times, so I suddenly found myself on a very high tier when I shouldn't really have been.

With ActiveCampaign, a subscriber is counted once whether they are on one list or ten, and it doesn't matter how many different ways you're communicating with them. That can make ActiveCampaign much cheaper in the long run than other systems.

The next panel, Contact Trend, shows you whether your list is growing or shrinking, which is a good test of your communication with them. If things are going well you're going to see a steady rise, and it'll tell you how many people have been added in the last period and what percentage that represents of the total. If you're doing badly—for example, if you send out an email that annoys a lot of people—then people will unsubscribe and you'll see a dip.

The third panel is a feed of corporate announcements from ActiveCampaign, which is an easy way of keeping up to date with new functionality, partnerships, etc. For example, on the day I took the screenshot above, ActiveCampaign were announcing Facebook custom audience integration.[1]

Below those panels, you can track the campaigns that have been going out and the automations that are running, as well as managing templates, which is how ActiveCampaign allows you to maintain a consistent look and feel to your emails.

When I log in, the key panels I look at are "All Contacts", "Contact Trend", and the timeline. For example, if I see someone has unsubscribed, I'll click through to their contact record and see why they unsubscribed. Sometimes, they'll tell you the reason or even leave a message. It's always worth checking that record. For example, a few days before I wrote this, I clicked on somebody who had unsubscribed, and they had left a message saying they were changing email addresses and asking me to resubscribe them with their new email address. I was able to give my assistant the details and I kept the subscriber. If I hadn't checked their record, I would have simply assumed they didn't want to hear from me again.

---

[1] If you run Facebook ads, you know how important retargeting is. Once somebody is on your list, they're an enthusiastic subscriber so you might as well remarket to them and stay in touch. ActiveCampaign allows you to add subscribers to a custom audience automatically. That cuts out a lot of the hard work of remarketing to people.

Key terms in ActiveCampaign

Now that we've seen the ActiveCampaign dashboard, let's review some terminology that you need to be familiar with. It's worth nothing that ActiveCampaign uses some words in ways that can be confusing if you're coming from another system like Aweber. If you're new to email marketing, however, you won't notice anything amiss: there's nothing to "unlearn", you just have to get used to the language.

List

In ActiveCampaign, a **list** is simply a collection of contacts that you have grouped together because you want to track or interact with them separately from other contacts in your database.[2]

For example, in my own system I have a separate list for each of my bribes. If someone downloads a copy of my free ebook *Sixteen Ways to Grow Your Business With a Book*, they go into a list called *16ways*. If they register for my webinar *Your Book is Your Brand*, they get added to a list called *YBIYB*. That way, when I want to send an email to everyone who read *Sixteen Ways*, I can just pick that list (I'll show you how to do that later), and no-one else has to get those emails.

---

[2] When I first started using ActiveCampaign, I came from a system where "list" referred to a collection of contacts *and all the pre-written messages that would be sent to those contacts over time*. So, when I moved across, I tied myself in knots until I got used to that idea.

Another way to achieve the same result — and this is the way many email providers do it — is by adding what's called a *tag*. If that's what you're used to, you may prefer to have a single master list of all contacts and tag users based on their behavior. The main reason I don't suggest that approach is that Active-Campaign's email sending process is based on lists rather than tags.

Automation

An **automation** in ActiveCampaign is a sequence of actions that you carry out over time — other systems call this a campaign, a funnel, or even a list!

The type of automation most people are familiar with (because, let's face it, we've all been through at least one of these at some point) is an email follow-up sequence: you opt in for a free bribe from someone's website, and a moment later an email arrives with the download link. The next day, another email arrives from them, then another a couple of days later, and over the next week or so, you continue to receive emails about that download.

That kind of automation is incredibly easy to set up in Active Campaign. However — and this is why I love and recommend the system — you can also create much more sophisticated sequences with text messages and even physical mail, and you can also set conditions to decide what happens to a specific contact (for example, you could set up a sequence where you send a postcard if someone is in the US, but substitute an email instead if they are in any other country).

> **Used to another system?**
>
> In many email systems, the list and the automation are the same thing. In Aweber, for example, when you create a list, you have to set up the sequence of emails that will be sent to people when they join that list. You can't separate the two.
>
> ActiveCampaign's approach is more flexible—and an automation can be triggered by lots of actions, not just signing up for a list. For example, you could start an automation for people who visit a specific page on your website or who click on a specific link in an email.

Campaign

How ActiveCampaign uses the word **campaign** was one of the most confusing aspects of the system when I switched.

In most other systems, "campaign" refers to what Active-Campaign calls an automation. In ActiveCampaign, it means an email!

The key distinction you need to get clear on in your mind is that a LIST is a group of people, a CAMPAIGN is an email, and an AUTOMATION is a series of steps that you perform on a contact

Creating your first list

With all of that out of the way, it's time to create our very first list.

Because automations and lists are separate in ActiveCampaign, you don't even need to know what you're going to do with the people on a list. You don't have to think about what bribes you'll give them. You don't have to know what emails you'll send them. You just need to know why you're singling them out. So, we are going to create a list called Reader Bonus which we will use—would you believe it!—when we build the Reader Bonus funnel.

To start a new list, you can go to the dashboard and click the down arrow next to "CREATE NEW CAMPAIGN". The fourth item on the menu that appears will be "CREATE A NEW LIST". Alternatively, you can click on the <Lists> link on the top menu on any page in ActiveCampaign.

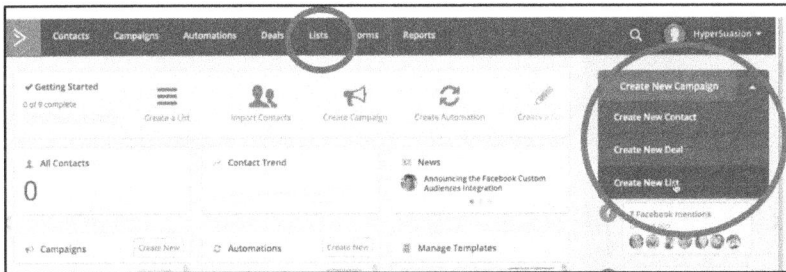

The first time you click on <Lists>, you'll see a page like this. For now, as you don't have any lists set up, it's empty and the only thing on the page is the link to "Create a new list". As you add lists, that will disappear, however the green button at the top that says [+ Add a New List] is always there, so click that now.

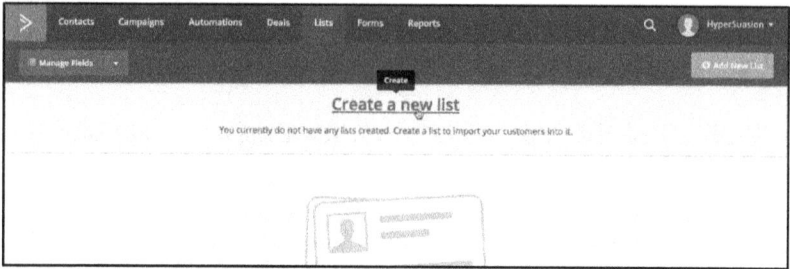

A new popup will appear that asks you for basic information about the list you're creating. You can see I've already filled this out.

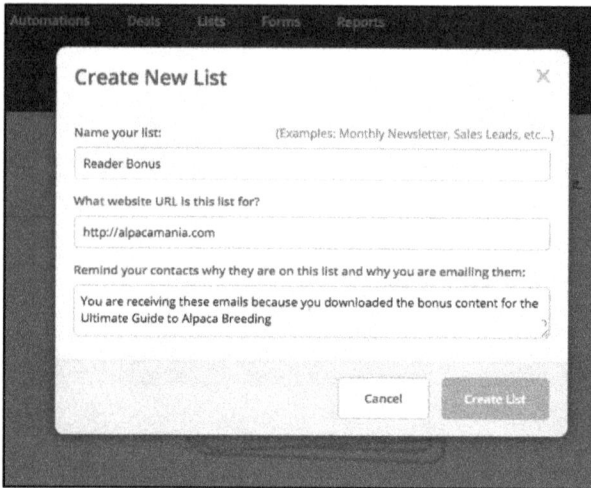

Name your list: This is the name that is used to identify your list. You'll see it in the Lists page, and it's also what your subscribers see, for example on the Unsubscribe page. So, make it meaningful. In this case, I've called it "Reader Bonus".

What website URL is this for: Next you're going to tell the system which specific website you are going to use this list with.

Remind your contacts why they are on this list and why you are emailing them: This is another piece of information that is primarily used when someone is about to unsubscribe. Let's face it, people will forget that they asked you to send them information, so it's useful that the system allows you to remind them why they thought it was a good idea. Since this list is for readers of a specific book, you're going to want to mention the book title and that that they joined so that they could download the bonus content.

Once you've filled in the form, click [Create Link] and you're done.

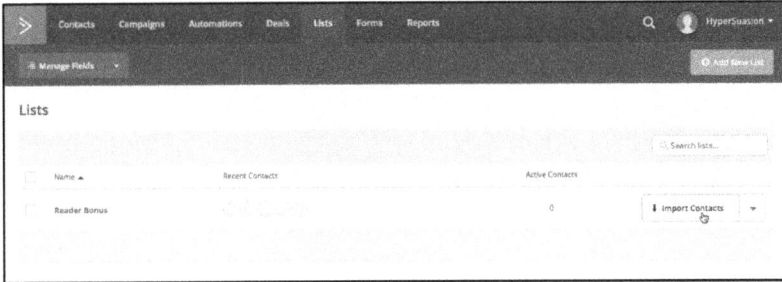

Now, if you were switching over from another system, you could click [Import Contacts] and upload a CSV file, but as this is a new list, you can ignore that for now.

Exercise

Create two lists in your email system

1)   Reader Bonus

2)   Free + Shipping

6

Contacts

In normal running, you're going to be letting ClickFunnels create contacts for you in your database, so you wouldn't be doing what we are about to do. However, I included this chapter for two key reasons.

First, we are going to need a dummy contact in the system so that we can continue to set things up and test.

Second, the screens for adding a contact are the same as the screens for editing a contact. I mentioned earlier in the book that it's useful to be able to go into a contact and see what they've been doing or update information like their telephone number or email address.

So, let's create a new contact.

First, click on < Contacts > on the top menu of the Active-Campaign window, then click on the green [+ New Contact] button.

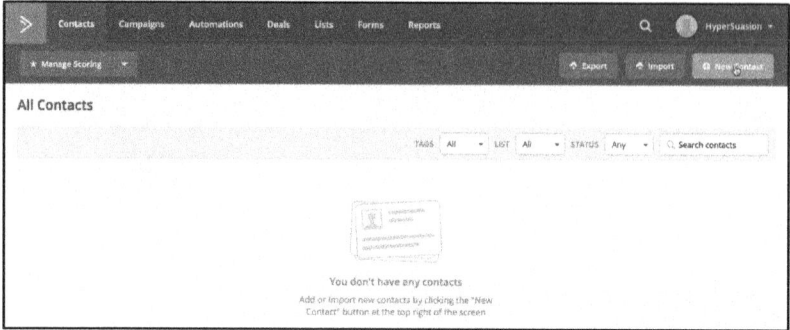

That brings up the new contact profile, where you'll enter details of the contact. You can safely ignore the "Organization" field—that's used for tracking the company that a lead works for, and we don't need it for these funnels.

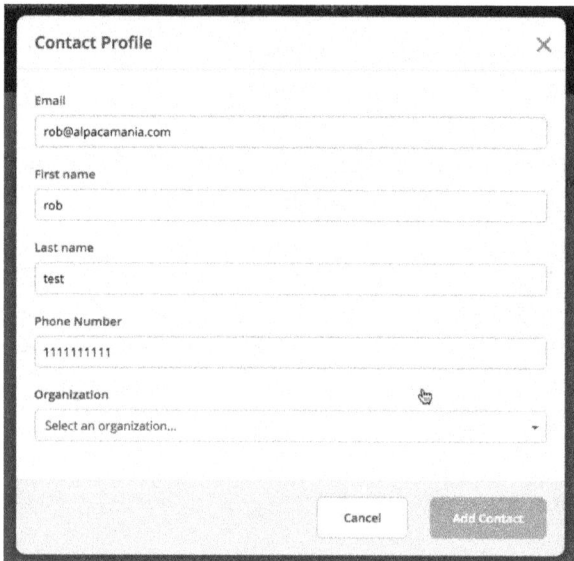

So, all you're going to do is enter an email address, first and last name, and you can either put in a telephone number or leave it blank for now. The details you see in the picture above are made up, but for this exercise I suggest you add yourself with a real email address that you'll be able to receive your test messages on.

When you click [Add Contact] a second screen comes up which allows you to carry out specific actions on the new contact. The first option you'll see is to add the contact to your lists. If you click the down arrow on the right, you'll see all the lists in your system. For this exercise, add yourself to both of the lists you created earlier (ignore the other options) and click [Apply].

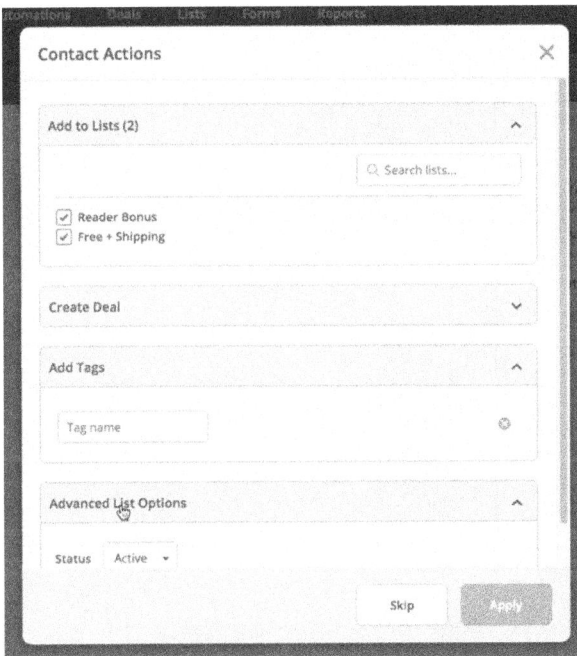

This will take you back to the "All contacts" screen, and you'll see that your new contact is now listed. Also, if you used a real email address and it's linked to an online avatar (for example, if you've created an avatar at Gravatar.com), Active-Campaign will fetch the associated image and add it to the contact record. That's a very useful function—in the past I've recognized people at live events because I'd seen their photo in my email system.

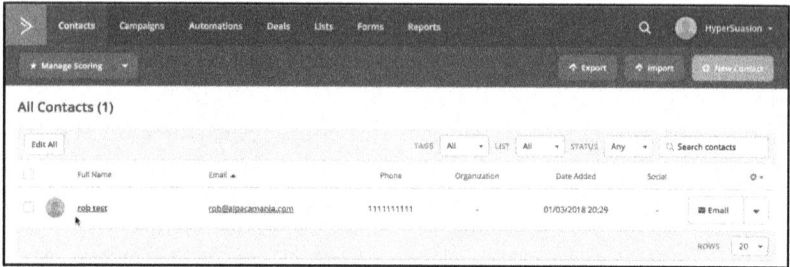

Now that you've got a contact set up, let's go into their record. In the All Contacts screen, click on the contact's name, This will take you into their profile.

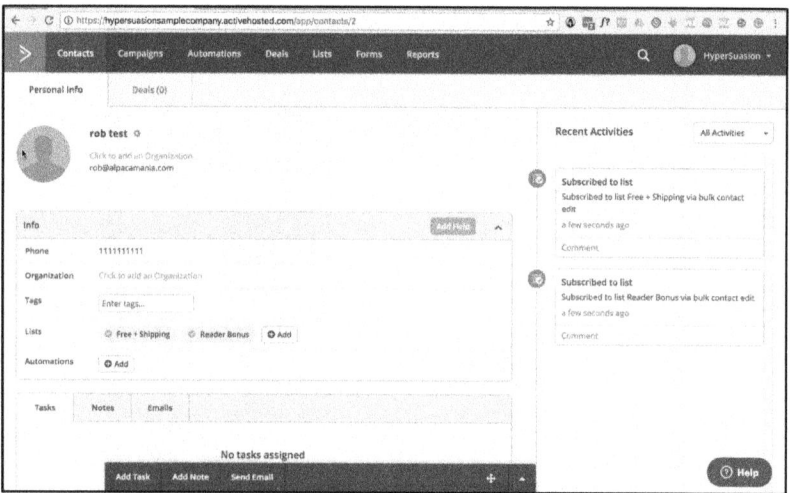

In this screen, you can see what lists a contact is subscribed to, whether they have been assigned any tags, and whether they are currently going through any automations.

You can also add notes about them and send them a personal email.

Down the right-hand side is a personal timeline where you'll be able to see what they've been doing: what emails have been sent to them, which emails they opened, what links they clicked, etc.

Exercise

If you haven't set up your contact yet, create a contact using your own details and add yourself to the Reader Bonus and Free + Shipping lists you created.

Now that you've got a contact set up, let's send an email!

7

Broadcast Emails

In email marketing, we differentiate between two types of emails, *broadcasts* and *autoresponders*.

Broadcasts are emails that go out to a group of contacts all at exactly the same time. For example, you might want to send out a "Happy Holidays" message to all your subscribers on 20th December.

Autoresponders are sent to a single contact in response to something that they did. For example, you might have an email that goes out five days after someone downloads a free report from your site.

In our funnels, we're primarily going to be using autoresponders because everything is driven by when people opt in. However, creating a broadcast email will allow me to teach you all the skills you need to create emails, so we'll start with that.

To create a broadcast email, click on <Campaigns> in the top menu.

The first time you do this, you'll see a screen that looks like this.

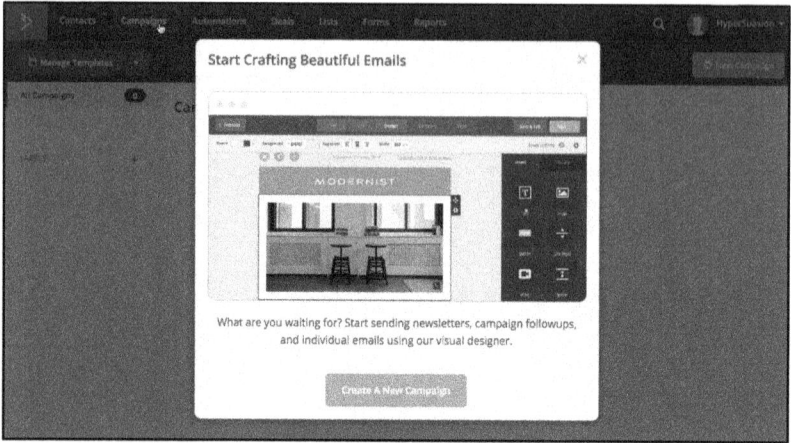

Click the green [Create A New Campaign] button.

That will take you into the first screen of the campaign wizard, where you will pick what type of message you want to create.

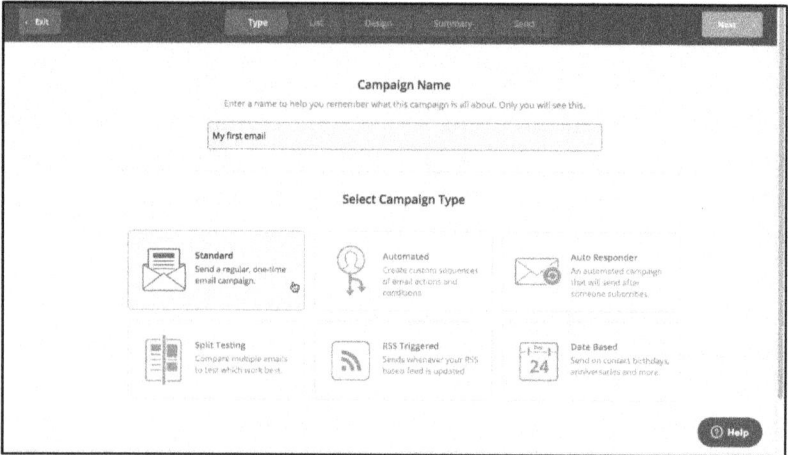

The first thing the system asks for is a name for the email. This is not the subject line; it's an internal name that only you will see, so you should use something meaningful that you'll recognize later.

Below this you'll see six campaign types.

The option we are going to use for this exercise is **Standard**, which is a regular one-time email campaign. In other words, what other systems call a broadcast.

Automated takes you to the automation wizard which we will be looking at in a later chapter,

Auto-Responder is a hangover from the days before Active-Campaign introduced automations. Originally, you would set up sequences email by email. "When someone joins this list send this email out on day 5." Then, you would create another email "When someone joins this list send this email on day 10." Everything appeared in one long list of all the emails that were set to go out ever to anyone and it was very confusing.

Automations are a much easier way to manage your sequences because they group all the relevant emails together and we can see a timeline of what's happening, so we don't use Auto-Responder anymore.

Split testing. If you're into split testing, you can set up multiple versions of a broadcast email and figure out which ones have the higher open rate, click-through rate, etc.

RSS triggered is great for sending emails each time you create a blog post.

Date-based emails are messages that you can set up to go out on people's birthdays, anniversaries, and so on. Obviously, you've got to be collecting that information in order to set these up.

In practice, the only type of email that I ever create in this screen is Standard, so highlight that and click [Next].

In the next screen, you're going to select which lists the email is going to be sent to.

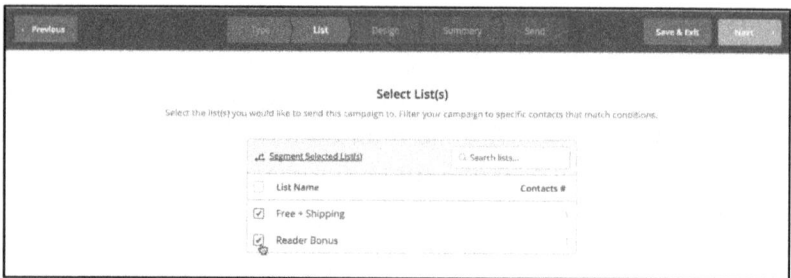

As you create more lists, this will become more useful. For example, if you have reader bonus lists for multiple books, you could send an email just to the readers of a specific book, or two related books. Or you can select every list (the checkbox to the left of List Name) and you'll send an email to every active contact in your database.

Once you've picked the specific lists you want to send an email to, click [Next] and you'll be taken to the next step of the wizard, which is the Design step.

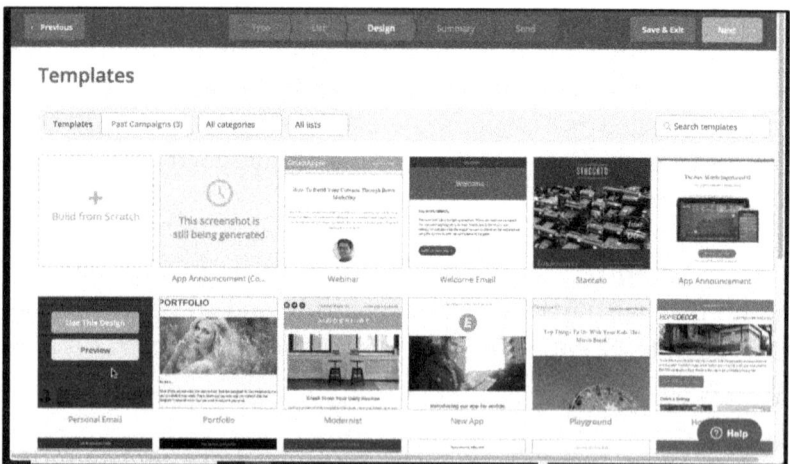

Here you have the option of building your email from scratch or using an existing template. Templates are how ActiveCampaign ensures that your emails look consistent, and once you've created an email that looks how you want it, you can turn it into a template and keep reusing it.

For the purposes of our demonstration, rather than starting from scratch we're going to take one of their existing templates — Personal Email.

What we're going to do is edit it and use it for our first broadcast. And then I'll show you how to save your own version of it to as a template that you can use for future emails.

If you click on [Preview], you can see what it will look like on a computer screen and on a mobile phone, and then you can click on [Use This Design] to create a new email based on the template.

That will open a screen which will ask you for a subject line. For now, we'll call it "Welcome to Alpaca Mania" and click [Continue].

That will take you into the email.

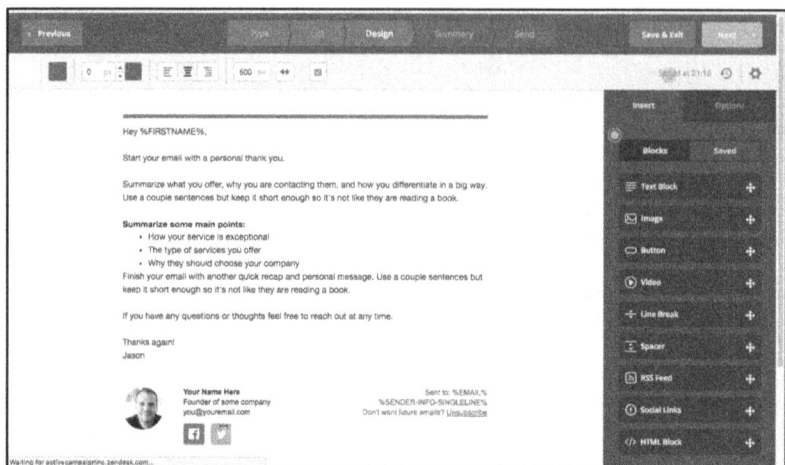

Before you create any content, let's edit the signature block at the bottom.

To change the photo, click it. A menu bar will appear, and the third button is [New Image]. Click that and upload your headshot.

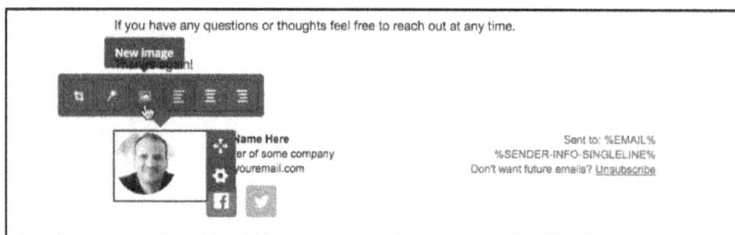

A word of caution about your headshot. On a computer, ActiveCampaign will scale the image to fit the frame it's in. On a phone or tablet, however, the image is scaled to fit the *screen*, so unless you want your face to be huge, you'll need to make sure the image is the right size before you upload it: about 80px by 80px is fine for the signature.

Once you've updated the image, you can edit the text by clicking on it and replacing it with your own details.

The block to the right gives people your unsubscribe link. That must be somewhere on the email, so you may as well leave it where it is.

Next, you'll want to update the social media icons. Start by clicking on the social media block — a menu will pop up.

There's a dropdown menu that allows you to switch between having the icons in a horizontal row or a vertical column.

To the left of that is an icon with three linked circles. Clicking that brings up a screen where you can enter your social media links.

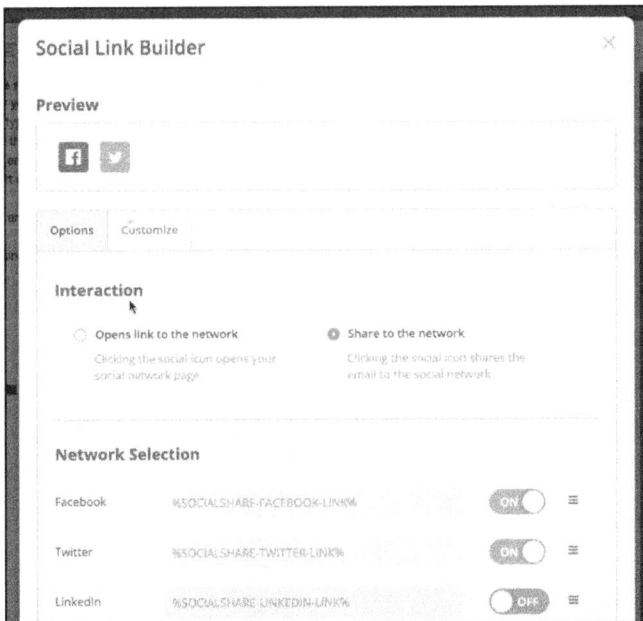

By default, this screen is set up for the links to be sharing links—in other words, they'll allow the user to share a copy of the email to their own social media. If you'd prefer to send readers to your own social media profiles and pages, click the left radio button ("Opens link to the network"). Unfortunately, you can't mix and match—you can't have some networks opening and others sharing—so pick which you prefer.

If you switch to "Opens link...", the urls will change, and you can go down the list and paste in your own links.

The On/Off switches let you select which icons will be displayed, and you can reorder the icons by clicking on the three horizontal lines on the right of each row and dragging it up or down.

The Customize tab allows you to alter the look of the icons.

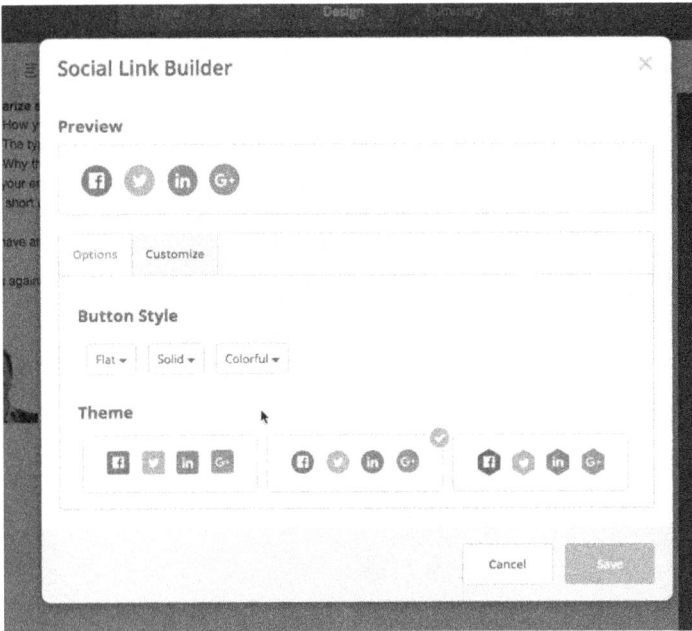

You can switch between flat or 3D (which adds a shadow), solid or outline, and colorful, dark or light.

Once you've finished editing the signature block, you can edit the text.

The most basic change you can make is to highlight the text that's currently there, delete it, and type in your own. We'll look at more complex editing when we discuss automation emails, but for now enter some simple text.

Hey %FIRSTNAME%,

I hope you like my first email.

To your success.

Rob

At the top right are two buttons, [Save & Exit] and [Next >]

If you click [Save & Exit] at this point, ActiveCampaign will simply save a draft and take you out to the list of campaigns.

Clicking [Next >] takes you to the Campaign Summary screen, where you can verify the details so far.

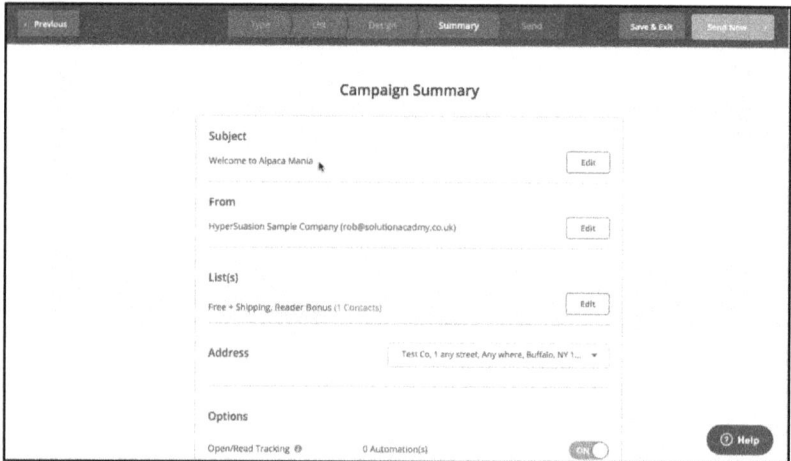

You can check that the subject is correct, and your company details. If you haven't set up your address yet, it will ask you to add a new one and it won't allow you to send an email until that's done.

You can also see which lists the email is being sent to, and how many contacts will receive it. If you've been following along, you'll notice something odd: you have two lists selected, but ActiveCampaign says it is only sending the email to one contact.

This is one of the features of ActiveCampaign that I love. If a contact is on multiple lists and you've selected those lists, they will only get the email once. That's a great way of avoiding "email fatigue" and reducing unsubscribes.

Note: This only works for lists that you select at the same time. If you were to send an email to a list then go back and send it to a different list (i.e. you hit "send" twice), anyone who is on both lists will get the email twice.

Next you have tracking and sending options. These are advanced features of ActiveCampaign, and allow you to add people to new automations based on their behavior.

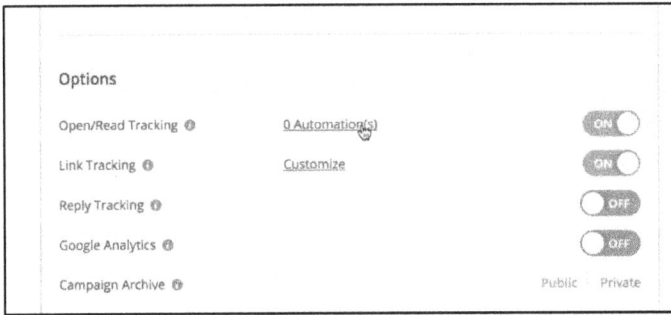

If you use Google Analytics, you can also add your tracking code to your emails.

And finally, there's the Campaign Archive, which allows you to share your emails into an archive of all your past campaigns. If these are marketing emails sent to a general audience there is absolutely no reason to keep them private, so you can leave it as Public.

The next option, Delivery, allows you to switch between sending the email immediately or setting a time and date in the future.

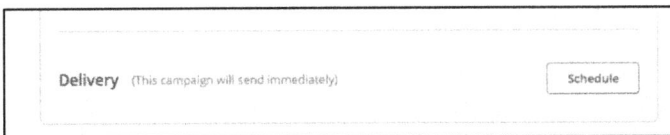

The next block of options will help you to check everything before you hit send.

Send Test Email	rob@solutionacadmy.co.uk	Send Test
Preview	Email Client Preview	Desktop Preview
Spam Check		✓ Passed

The two most important options here are "Send Test Email", which allows you to send a copy of the email to your own inbox. It's worth doing that and then checking it on your computer, phone, and tablet. When you click [Send], it will warn you that you are sending it to yourself, but you can click [Send Anyway]. (If you find that your test emails aren't getting through, it's because your email client doesn't like the fact you are emailing yourself and it's blocking them or putting them in the Junk folder).

Spam check, as the title suggests, checks the content and subject line for any features that internet service providers might consider spammy.

Ignore the two Preview options as they are a paid extra (unless you're on one of the top-level subscriptions).

Once you've checked your test message, you can either click [Send Now] and have the email go immediately, or click the [Schedule] button and set a future time and date, as I said above.

If you do decide to schedule the email for later, you'll see the [Send Now] button changes to [Finish]. Clicking that takes you to a screen that confirms the sending schedule.

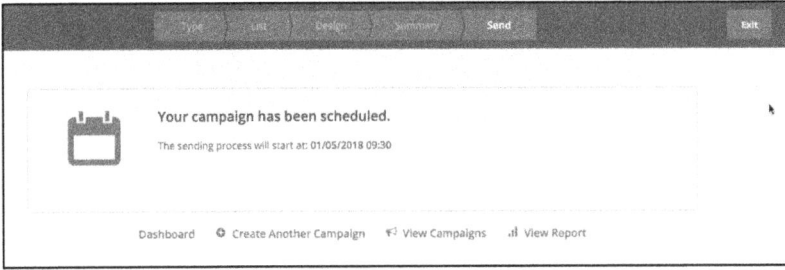

Click [Exit] to go back to the dashboard.

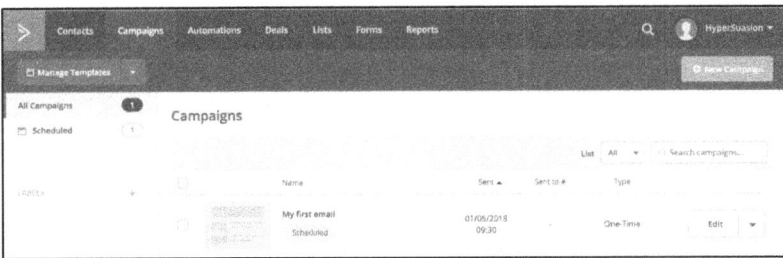

Saving a template

You put a lot of work into editing the signature block, so it would be good to save that for future use. You can do that by clicking the down arrow next to Edit on the right.

The Duplicate option makes a single copy of the email as a draft. That's useful if you want to use a past email as the starting point for your new email—for example, each month I tell members of my Author Expert Insiders Mastermind about the next session by copying the previous month's email and updating it.

If you have created a standard email that you want to use as the basis for future emails regularly, for example your newsletter, then it's better to save it as a template. Simply click "Save as Template" and it will be added to the templates list.

Exercise

If you haven't done it yet, set up a simple broadcast email and update the signature block.

Save the email as a template.

8

Automations

Now that we've created a single email, let's look at how we put emails and other actions together into an automation.

As I said before, an automation is a list of actions that are going to take place based on when something—a trigger action—happens such as someone joining a list, downloading something, or buying a product.

A key feature that I'll show you later is the ability to send a message to someone other than the contact, for example your assistant. This is critical for the Free + Shipping funnel, because it's how you'll know that someone has bought your book and you need to send it to them.

Examples of automations:

- A follow-up sequence when someone opts in
- Messages to someone who buys your product
- A message to your VA to ship your book to a new subscriber
- An SMS sent to someone when they register for your webinar

If you upgrade to higher levels of ActiveCampaign, you can also send SMS messages to a contact's cellphone as part of your campaign. With email inboxes getting so full, that's a very powerful and immediate way to get someone's attention.

The Indoctrination Sequence

For this book, our basic strategy will be

1) Each funnel will have its own automation
2) New contacts will also be added to an additional "best of the best" sequence—what Ryan Deiss of Digital Marketer calls an Indoctrination Sequence

99% of the automations you create in ActiveCampaign, at least initially, will be what I call "straight line automation": in other words, the most complicated thing that happens is that you wait a few days between steps.

ActiveCampaign has the facility to create far more sophisticated automations with different paths based on all sorts of conditions and behaviors, but we're focusing on the basics in this book and keeping things simple.

So, let's start by creating your Indoctrination Sequence.

From the ActiveCampaign dashboard, click <Automations> on the top menu. The first time you do that, you'll get a splash screen with a green button at the bottom labelled [Create A New Automation]. Click that. If you are on the Automations page instead, you can click the green [+ New Automation] button in the top right corner.

The automation wizard starts by offering you a range of pre-configured automations. Some of these are free, others are payable.

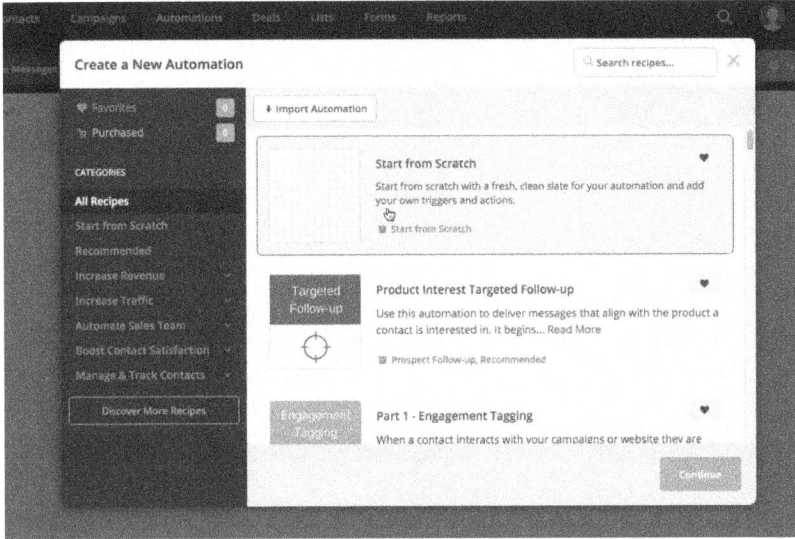

Since our automations are going to be simple, however, you can just click "Start from Scratch" then [Continue].

Triggers

Immediately, you'll be asked how a contact will enter the automation, and there are 23 options (which tells you something about the flexibility and power hidden under the hood of ActiveCampaign!).

The most common is **Subscribes to a list**, however you can see that there are also options for adding people who open and read an email, click on a link in an email, visit a page on your website (which requires additional setup on the site to allow ActiveCampaign to track what your contacts are doing there), and many other options based on their behavior and level of engagement.

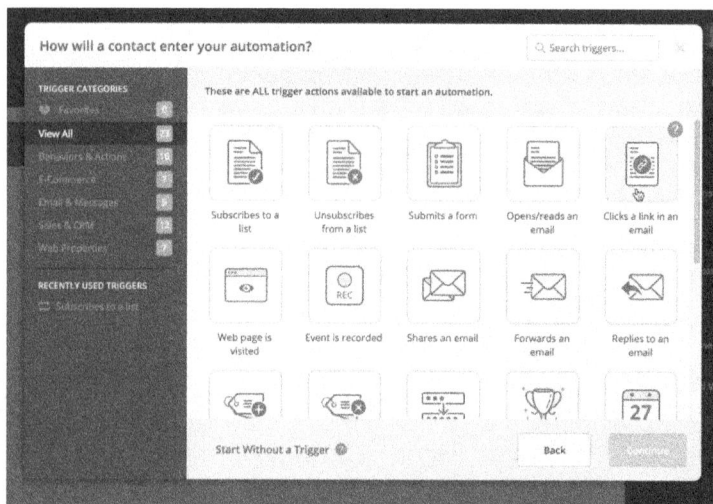

There's also an extremely useful trigger at the bottom of the screen, **Start Without a Trigger**. It allows you to set up automations that are triggered from within other automations so that you can "funnel stack" (put contacts through multiple funnels as they take more and more action). For example, when someone finishes an automation, you can decide what automation to put them through next based on information that you've gathered about them.

For now, keep things simple and pick **Subscribes to a List**, at which point the system will ask you to pick a list.

Normally, you would pick the specific list that was associated with the funnel that the automation is for. However, because this is an Indoctrination Sequence and we want to put all our contacts through it, _for this automation only_ you are going to pick **Any list**.

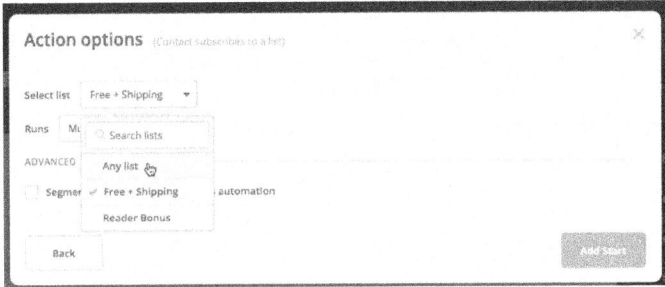

The next option, **Runs**, determines whether a contact is allowed to go through the automation several times (and get all
the messages each time) or only once.

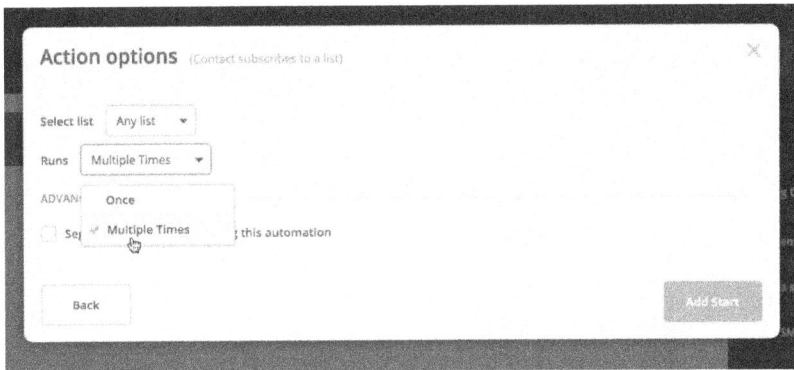

For most funnels, I set this to **Multiple Times**. That way, if a
contact wants to download your free report again, they can get
it. For the indoctrination sequence, however, I recommend you
set it to **Once**.

We're not talking about segmentation in this book, so as
soon as you've set the choices to "Any List, Once" you can click
on [Add Start].

Exercise

If you haven't done it yet, set up your Indoctrination Sequence auto-mation up to the point where you select and configure the trigger.

Actions

On the next screen, you will be asked to pick what happens when someone joins the automation.

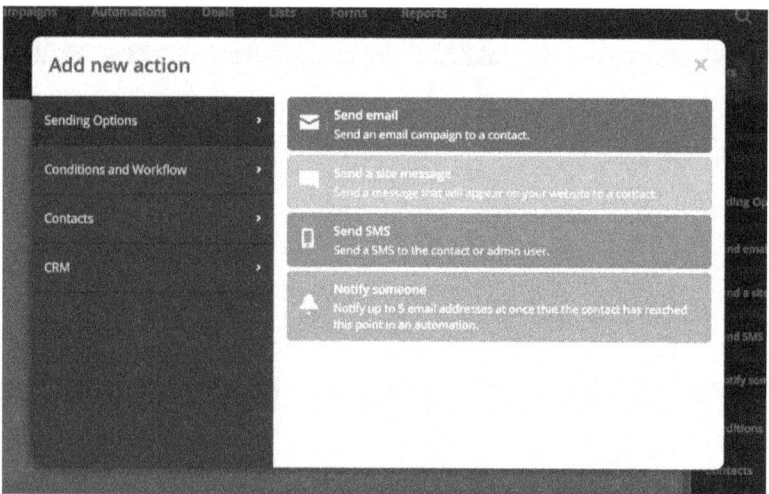

There are many different types of action that you can put in-to an automation.

The three tabs you'll find yourself in most of the time are "Sending Options", which are about sending messages; "Conditions and Workflow", which allow you to make choices about what happens next; "Contacts", which allows you to change the contact's record in the database (for example to add new infor-mation); and finally options to manipulate the CRM, which on-ly apply at higher subscription levels so we won't cover them here.

Sending Options

Most of the time (at least until you get more adventurous and advanced) your automations are going to be built around two basic actions: send an email, wait, send another email, wait some more, and so on.

So, in the Sending Options, 90% of the time you'll be clicking **Send Email**. The other main option you'll use in this tab is **Notify Someone**, which we'll look at when we build the Free + Shipping automation.

Conditions and Workflow

The Conditions and Workflow tab lets us specify what must happen before a subscriber moves from one step to the next.

The most useful option in this tab, for now at least, is **Wait**. This allows you to set a delay of a specific period (in minutes, hours, days, months, or even years) or to wait until a specific condition is met (for example, you could hold someone in an automation until they've replied to the last email—we used this when some of our clients asked us to help them make their funnels GDPR-compliant).

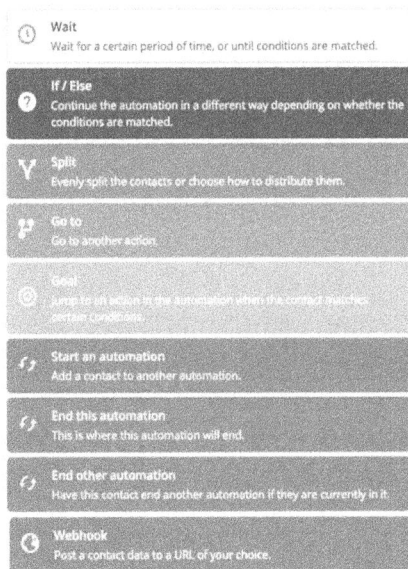

If/Else is another useful condition. I've used this, for example, to send different messages to people based on where they lived, or whether they had bought a specific product.

The other options are more advanced than you need for setting up the funnels in this book, so we'll ignore them for now.

Contacts

The Contacts options allow you to manipulate the contact record. So, based on their behavior, you could subscribe them to or remove them from a list. You can also change the information you have recorded about them, add or remove tags, add notes, and — at higher subscription levels — add or remove them from a Facebook custom audience.

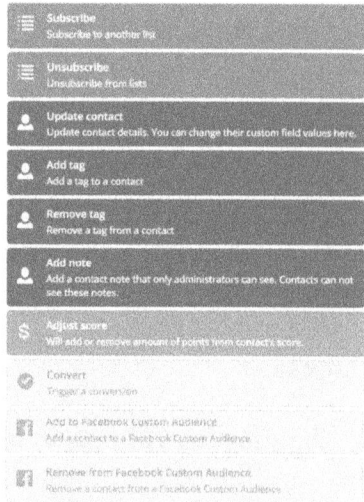

For now, go back to "Sending Options" and click on **Send Email**.

As we haven't created any emails yet for this automation, that will bring up a screen like this:

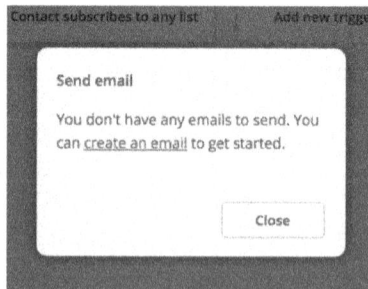

Setting up the Indoctrination Sequence

The idea of the indoctrination sequence is to turn strangers into fans. We're only going to run it for new subscribers, and there's nothing being sold in this sequence except you. So, we're going to send a welcome email and then 3-5 further emails over the next week with links to your best materials.

Choosing your best content

The point is to give them content that proves how skilled and knowledgeable you are without them having to keep opting in. It's basically five emails that say "Here's a really great article that I wrote about so and so," "Here's a great interview that I did."

Exercise

Make a list of your best content

- Blog posts
- YouTube videos you've created
- Facebook live videos
- Tools
- Checklists
- Infographics
- Assessments
- Diagnostics
- A free report
- Case studies

- Links to articles you've had published on other sites

- Links to podcast interviews that you've done

- Anything else you can think of

What else could you create easily and quickly? Add that to the list.

Pick 3-5 pieces of content from the list that best represent who you are and what you do.

Creating the Indoctrination Sequence

This is what the finished indoctrination sequence will look like:

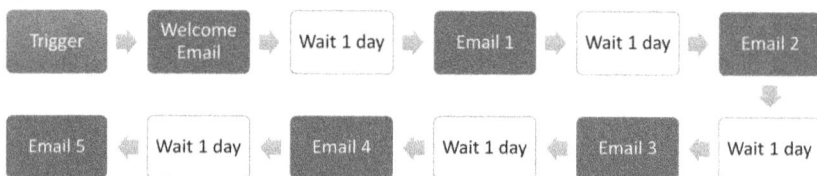

There's an initial trigger (which we've already said is that someone joins any of your lists), and a welcome email that gets sent immediately. Then you wait one day and send another email, and you repeat that cycle over 3-5 days.

I have seen some people put a loop at the end of their indoctrination sequence to wait for a year and then put people through it again from the start. Some audiences respond well to that, but others may not like it. So, if you plan to do that, test it and see what happens in a year's time.

To keep things simple, we're going to let people drop out of our automation at the end of it.

> **NOTE:** Because lists and automations ae separate, even when someone drops out of an automation, they stay in their original list. So, unless someone deliberately unsubscribes from a list that they are in, you will still be able to identify who, for example, bought your Free + Shipping offer.

The Welcome email

In the welcome email, you do several things.

1. Introduce yourself—who you are, how you're going to be able to help them, what change you're going to create for them as they work with you, etc.
2. Tell them about your blog or podcast, and how often you update it.
3. Set expectations about how often they're going to be hearing from you in general.
4. You want to end up in their inbox, not their spam or the dreaded Gmail Promotions tab (where emails go to die), so ask them to whitelist your emails. And it helps if you tell them what they're going to miss out on if they don't do that.
5. Give them links to your social media profiles and tell them to go and join you there, particularly any relevant Facebook pages or groups that you run.
6. Because they are getting added to this Indoctrination Sequence alongside the main information they requested from you, you should also let them know that they're going to get multiple emails from you. Tell them that you're going to be adding them to a special series of emails with great content, and warn them that some days they may get two emails on the same day from you, but it's only for the next five days.

7. Finally, at the end of the email I like to invite them to engage with you by replying with the answer to a simple question.

So, let's see what that looks like in practice.

Hi, I'm Jane Doe, CEO of Alpaca Mania, and I'm so excited you welcome you to our family. I know this is absolutely going to transform your income from alpaca breeding.

Here's what you can expect from us.

We add new episodes to our podcast Alpacas for Fun and Profit (LINK) twice a week, on Tuesdays and Fridays. Each time we do, I'll email you to let you know a new episode is ready for you, with a short description and why I think you'll benefit from listening.

From time to time, we'll also email you with news about new expert alpaca breeding courses, products, and other cool premium resources that will help you.

Sounds good? Great!

Before you go any further, here's a few actions you need to take right now.

If our emails aren't getting through to you, you're going to miss out on all the benefits of being an Alpaca Mania subscriber, so the first thing to do is to whitelist all emails from AlpacaMania.com and Jane Doe.

If you use Gmail, make sure you drag any emails from AlpacaMania.com or Jane Doe into the Priority Inbox. That way you won't miss anything from us.

Join us at our Facebook page (INSERT URL). This is our main way of communicating with our fans outside of email, and you'll often find me on there, answering questions or doing live videos.

That's all for now. I'm looking forward to helping you create a real alpaca explosion!

Jane Doe

CEO, Alpaca Mania

P.S. The next few days are going to feel like Christmas and your birthday all rolled up in one. Why? Because I'm going to send you some additional emails with links to some of my best online resources: articles, interviews, videos and other fantastic tools that will transform how you think about alpacas! It does mean that on a couple of days in the next week you may be getting two emails a day from me, but you're going to love what I've got for you. The first one will come tomorrow. It's an interview I did on the Alpaca Magic podcast, where I shared five things you should NEVER do to your alpacas! Stay tuned!

P.P.S. If you've got a second, I'd love to know your biggest question about raising alpacas. Just hit reply to this email, or shoot me a quick email at **jane@alpacamania.com**

Creating the Welcome Email

It's time to create your Welcome email.

Head back to ActiveCampaign. We left it at this screen:

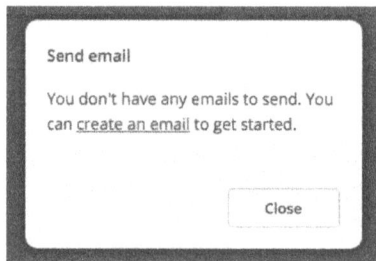

Click on Create an Email, which will take you to a screen that asks for a name for the email (just like when we created a broadcast). Call the email "Welcome" — and remember, this isn't the same as the subject line, your contacts won't see it.

From this point on, the process is similar to creating a broadcast, with minor differences because we don't need to decide who to send the email to or when.

On the next screen ActiveCampaign will ask you what template you want to use, and you'll see that the template you saved earlier is now available for you, so choose that.

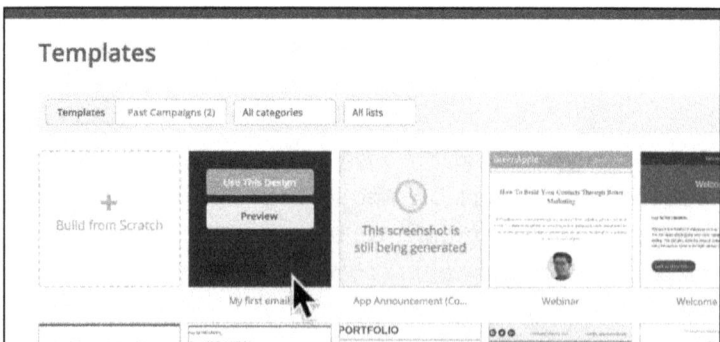

Next, it will ask you to confirm the sender details and to enter the subject that the contact will see.

When you've entered it, click on [Continue] and you'll be taken to the email editor, which is exactly the same as before, but it should have your details in the signature box.

You can highlight the text of the main message, delete it, and replace it with the text of your welcome email.

If you're not ready to create a proper email for your business yet, or if you just want a sample text you can use as the basis for yours, you can download the text of the welcome email above from **www.brightflamebooks.com/FunnelBonus**

If you know how to use a word processor then you'll get used to the main editor very easily. I also have a video course based on this book where I demonstrate how to use the editor in more detail. You can find out about it at

www.brightflamebooks.com/FunnelBonus

Personalizing Your Emails

I like to include the reader's name in my emails, and that's very simple to do in ActiveCampaign. You can add their first name just by typing the shortcode %FIRSTNAME% wherever you want it to appear.

You have a lot of shortcodes available in the system that will take information from the contact's profile and insert it into your messages. All you need to do is put the cursor wherever you want the information to appear and click Personalize on the menu bar.

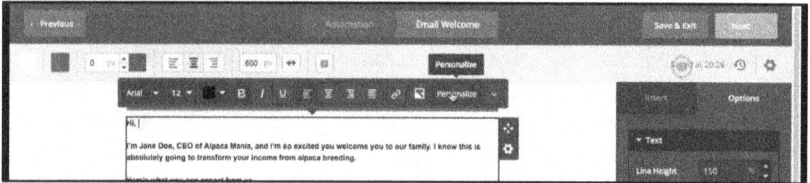

That will open a window with all the available choices, and you can click whichever one you want to add to your message.

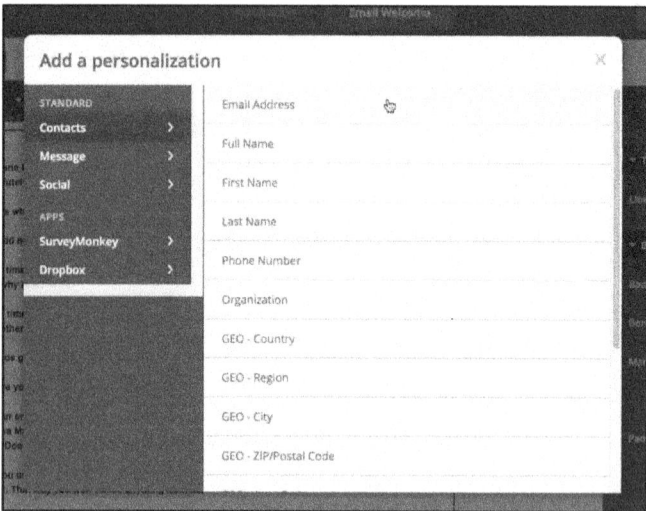

Once you're happy with your text, click the green [Next button] and you'll be taken to the campaign summary. This is similar to the broadcast email we created earlier, but without the scheduling options or the list of who it's being sent to.

Check the subject—if you want to change it, you can just click [Edit]—and send yourself a test email. If you're happy, click [Finish] and your first follow-up email is done.

You'll end up back at the overview of the automation. To set a name for the automation, click in the top left (where it says "Name your automation here") and type "Indoctrination Sequence".

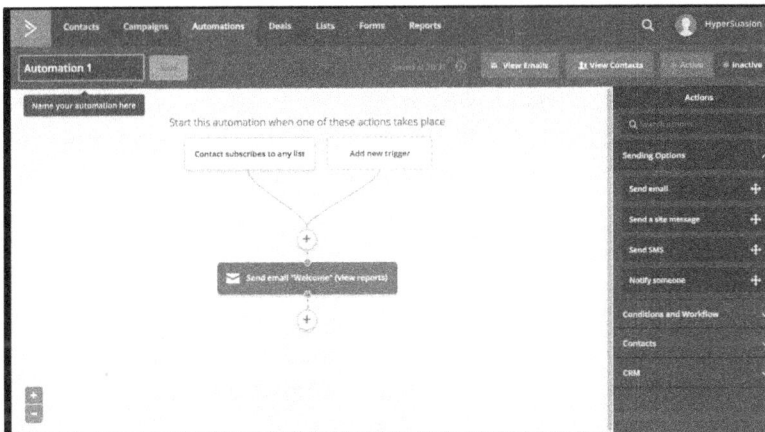

Adding a delay

Our next task is to add a one-day wait.

In the overview screen, you'll see that between each step there's a plus sign in a circle, and one at the bottom.

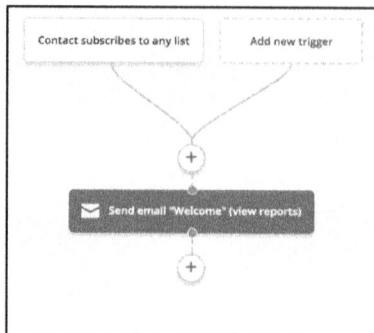

If you click on one of those circles, it will open up the Actions window and you can add a step. So, if you wanted to insert a step before the Welcome email goes out, you'd click the circle above it, and to add a step at the end of the automation, click the circle at the end.

We're going to add a wait after the Welcome email goes out, so click the final circle. On the Actions window, go to the Conditions and Workflow tab, choose Wait and set a 1-day delay.

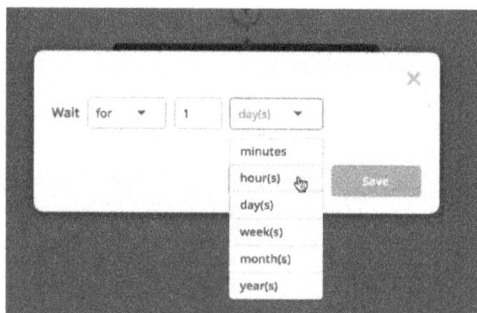

Once you've done that, you're all set.

Exercise

Set up your welcome email and add a one-day delay after it.

9

Making your Automation live

If you want contacts to start going through the activation, you'll need to turn it on.

If you look at the top right of the automation overview, you'll see two buttons marked [Active] and [Inactive]. Right now, the [Active] button is dimmed, and [Inactive] is highlighted.

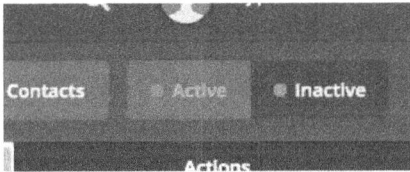

To turn the automation on, simply click [Active].

You can make it inactive again any time you need to by coming back to this page and clicking [Inactive].

Making an automation inactive is like hitting the pause button.

Once you've got your funnel up and running, if you need to make changes—to add or remove steps, or to change the order—it's a good idea to pause it while you work.

While it's paused, any contacts who are currently going through the automation will stay in whatever step they were in, and if they were in a Wait step, the system will remember how long they had been in there when you hit pause.

So, pausing the automation will protect you from any mistakes you make while you work.

New contacts won't join the automation while it's paused, even if they meet the trigger condition, so don't keep the automation paused for too long.

And remember to hit [Active] again when you're done!

Email 1

Our next task is to set up the follow-up emails in our sequence.

Here's an example of the kind of email you'll want to add:

Subject: Here's your free gift (1 of 5)

Hi (firstname)

Yesterday, I promised to send you one of our three most popular resources...

Before I do that, though, I wanted to take a moment to introduce myself.

{Insert personal photo}

That's a pic of me with my very first alpaca, Flossie. If only I'd known then what I know now! I'd always wanted to race alpacas, so getting Flossie was a dream come true for me, and now that you're a subscriber, I want to help you make your alpaca dreams come true for you, too!

Anyway, now that we're not strangers anymore, here's the first link

{insert link to content 1}

This is the podcast interview I promised to send you.

I know you're going to love it. The interviewer got me to share the top 5 things you should never do to your alpacas if you want them to be happy!

Talk soon.

Jane Doe

P.S. If you haven't joined the conversation over at my Facebook page, head over to XXX and join the fun!

That's our sample indoctrination email.

It includes a photo, so I need to show you how to add an image to your emails. Adding personal photos of yourself to these emails is a nice touch. Remember, these people have never met you before, and they're joining your list for the first time. Letting them into your world through pictures turns you into a real, multidimensional person that they can relate to.

Start by clicking the ⊕ at the end of the sequence and add a new email, using your template as before.

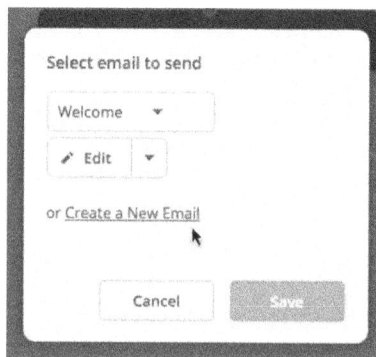

When you set up these emails, give them meaningful names that you'll recognize in the system. For example, this one would be something like "Email 1 – Top 5 podcast".

Give it the subject "Here's your free gift (1 of 5)" – obviously, if you chose fewer than 5 strong pieces of content, then it will be "1 of" however many you are going to send.

For the content, start by pasting in the text up to the point where you want to insert the image.

Next, you need to add a block for the image to go into.

Over on the right is a panel with two panes "Insert" and "Options". If the Insert pane isn't visible, click it and it will appear.

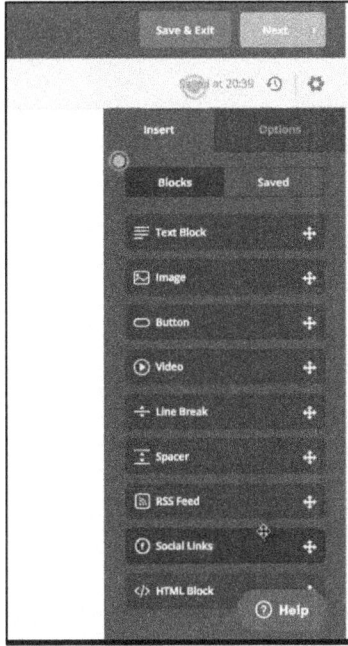

These tools allow you to add different types of content to your email. We want to add an image, so click [Image] and drag it left, over the main editing pane. As you move the mouse near the edges of the current content, you'll see a green line appear. This tells you where the image block is going to be inserted.

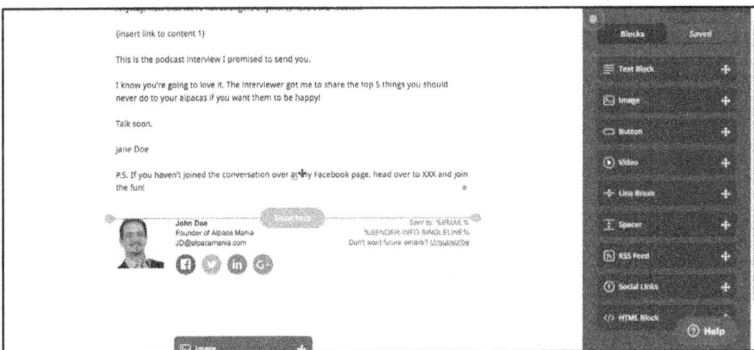

When the green line is across the bottom of the text block, let go of the mouse button and the image block will be inserted.

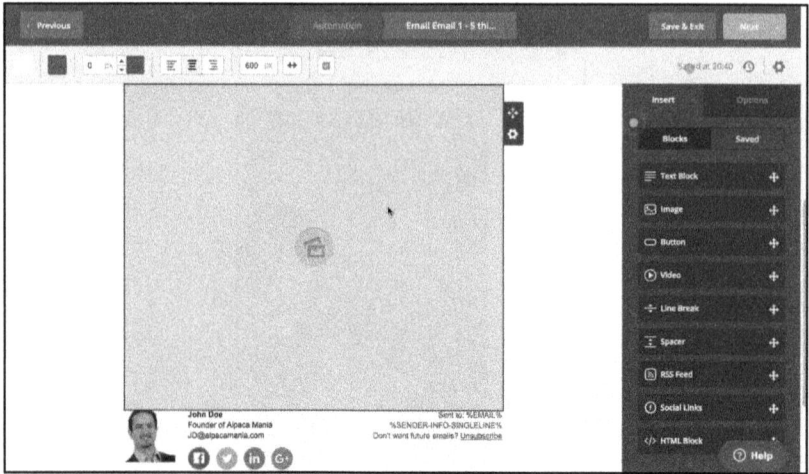

Adding an image is just like adding a photo to your signature block, so I won't repeat those instructions here. And as I said before, it's best to edit the image to be how you want it before you add it to your email.

To add the rest of the email text, the process is very similar. From the Insert pane, select [Text Block] and drag it over until the green line is below the image. Release the mouse button and the text block will be inserted.

Paste the rest of your text into the new text box and format it how you want it.

When you're done, click next and you'll go to the campaign summary screen. As always, I suggest sending yourself a test.

Exercise

Add your first 'best' of email.

Add a one day wait

Repeat for the other emails in the sequence.

PART THREE

Setting Up The Reader Bonus Funnel

10

The Reader Bonus Funnel

Now that we have some lists and our first automation set up in ActiveCampaign, in this chapter we are going to look at the first of our core funnels, the **Reader Bonus funnel**. We are starting with this one because it is the easiest of the funnels to create and, if you're not proficient with ClickFunnels, it's a good way to get started using the software.

The big idea behind this funnel is to start building a list of people who have bought your book.

The problem we face as authors is that when someone buys your book through a retail channel—whether on Amazon, Barnes and Noble, or anywhere else—you have no way of finding out who they are because retailers won't share that information with you.

The reader bonus funnel is simply a way of driving people to a lead capture page where they can give you their contact details so that you can start a conversation with them.

That's important because if someone has gone to the trouble of doing that, it's because they found the book content valuable and they want to take another step.

Think about it in terms of the Client Journey.

Your reader has gone to Amazon (Visitor), they were interested by your book (Suspect), and having read it, they are now educated on you and your solution. So Amazon is holding a list of your Prospects. But in order to move them into further stages, you are going to have to direct them to your site and get them interested and educated again.

Where it fits
(The Client Journey)

To do that, you need a call to action in the book that leads to your funnel. The big picture is this.

The Big Picture

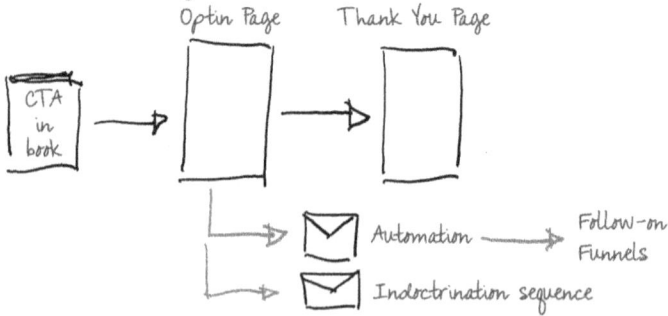

If you don't have a call to action in your book at the moment, all is not lost. If your book is self-published through Kindle, Createspace, Ingram Spark, or companies like that, it's easy enough to add a call to action to an existing book. If your book was published through one of the vanity publishing companies, you may find that they charge a substantial fee for updates. If you published with a hybrid publisher, you'll need to check their terms.[3]

And of course, if you published with BrightFlame Books, you and I will have had a serious conversation about calls to action early on and we will have planned them well before your book was published!

Thinking of publishing, launching, or relaunching a book?

Take a look at how we can help you with an existing book:

www.brightflamebooks.com/yourbooklaunch

So, you can add your call to action into an existing book and send readers to an optin page where they will give you their email address, and from there you send them to a thank you page where you deliver the bonuses you promised in the book.

At the same time, you're going to add them to two automations: the Indoctrination Sequence you set up in the last section (if this is the first time they've made contact with you), and an-

---

[3] Unfortunately, if you are "traditionally" published (through one of the Big 5 or one of their imprints) you will probably find it very hard to get changes made to a book that is already in circulation.

other sequence which is designed to encourage them to buy other products and services.

One of my big beliefs in business is that "a buyer is a buyer" and it doesn't matter whether they've bought a $20 book, a 99-cent ebook, or a $500 product: they're much more likely to buy something else from you than someone who's never bought anything. Someone who has read one of your books is very likely to buy your next book (as long as you wrote a good first book!). They are also very likely to buy your products and programs. So, if you can find out who your book buyers are, you are identifying very high value leads.

> **Why You Want One**
>
> Book buyers are most likely to buy your next book. They are also likely to buy products and services ("a buyer is a buyer is a buyer...").
>
> BUT Bookstores won't tell you who bought your book

In Summer 2018, I was in San Diego helping one of my clients, legendary marketer Bill Glazer, to run a live 2-day event based on his book.

At the event, one of the attendees, JP, came up to introduce himself. He had bought my book *Premium!* soon after it was released. He then bought the product I promoted in that book, *VIP Day Instant Income Secrets*, as well as all my other books.

And when he saw me promoting Bill's event and saw that I was going to be speaking at the event, he bought a ticket *and flew 5000 miles across the Atlantic, from Finland to San Diego* to meet me. A few weeks later, he became a coaching client.

A buyer is a buyer (is a buyer, is a buyer…).

What you need

In order to set up your Reader Bonus Funnel, you are going to need the following:

1. A compelling bonus stack
2. A cover image or 3D image of your book
3. A follow-up email sequence
4. An Amazon listing that converts
5. Reviews
6. One (or more) calls to action in your book

The first critical component is your bonus stack. In other words, you need some bribes to give away in exchange for their contact details.

Here, for example, is the bonus stack for *Premium!*

As a thank you for buying this book I'd like to give you some free gifts. Simply visit

http://premiumpricingbook.com

and confirm your purchase to get access to:

- ✅ "Premium Pricing Secrets": a LIVE recording in front of members of a $20,000 mastermind group, in which I share my deepest, darkest secrets on how to charge more
- ✅ MP3 download of the whole event, so you can listen in the car, in the gym, on the train, or wherever you want
- ✅ Download the entire slide deck so you can follow along as I take the group through my Premium Pricing Secrets

---

When it comes to your bonuses, there are many possibilities, but whatever you choose has to be linked to the content of your book.

- Worksheets/Workbook
- Multi-day course or challenge
- Audio version of the book
- Videos
- Infographics
- Other books/ebooks

An easy bonus to create is a set of **worksheets** for each chapter or even an entire **workbook**. You can do that very simply by taking exercises that you would have put into the book and moving them into a separate downloadable document. You don't even have to remove the exercises from the book itself. Many people don't like to write in print books, and obviously you can't write in an ebook, so readers will appreciate a separate printable workbook or worksheets.

A further development of this idea is to use those exercises as the basis for a multi-day **challenge** or turn the content of the book into a short **product**.

Many people like to listen to books as they exercise or drive, so an **audiobook** version of your book can be a great bonus. Hiring experienced voice talent can be expensive. However, you can record yourself reading your own book using a high-quality microphone plugged into your smartphone or computer. And you can always sell the audiobook separately as a product in its own right.

The help area for ACX—Amazon's audiobook publishing platform—has many useful articles to help you plan and produce your audiobook. You can find it at https://audible-acx.custhelp.com/.

When it comes to **videos**, one very simple approach (which I learned from Tamara Monosoff) is to record a short summary of each chapter and use those videos as the bonus. One of my writing and publishing clients took this idea a little further and had every chapter of her book turned into a short whiteboard animation.

Another way of summarizing the content of your books is to create **infographics**. Here, for example, is part of a summary infographic of the Stephen R Covey's classic 7 Habits of Highly Successful People (http://bit.ly/2M3p2e6).

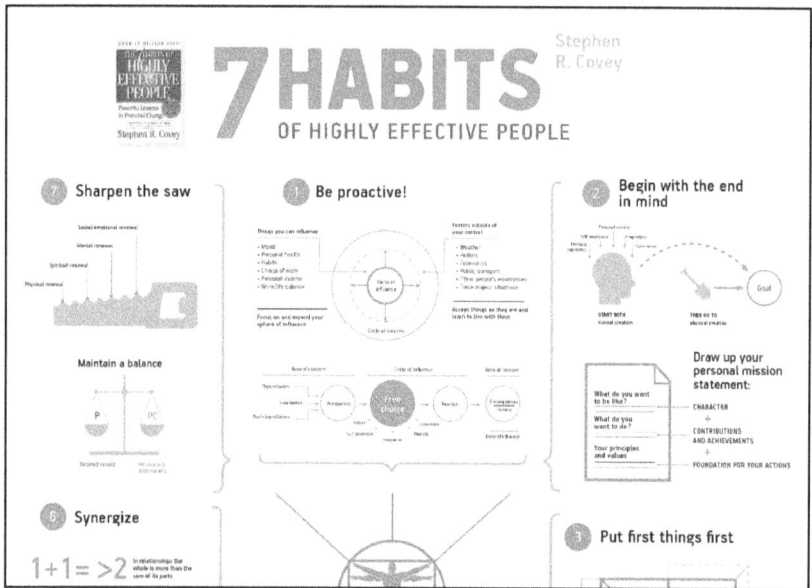

And of course, you can always offer other **books and ebooks** — either in full or as excerpts — as part of the bribe.

The key is that if you want people to register, you have to provide value and ideally your bribe should lead to the next step you want people to take.

Exercise

If you don't currently have a call to action in your book, or if you have one but you want to update it:

1) What materials do you already have that you could offer as a bonus to readers?

2) What could you create quickly?

3) Why would readers want these bonuses? How do the bonuses help them to solve their problem or achieve their (book-related) goals?

Your Cover Image

You're also going to need a cover image or a 3D image of your book. If you don't have a 3D image of your book, you can get someone to create one quite cheaply from freelancer sites like Fiverr.com.

Here, for example, is a 3D mockup of *Premium!* I use it everywhere: on sales pages, optin pages, in my email signature, and anywhere else I need it. I also have similar images for all my other books.

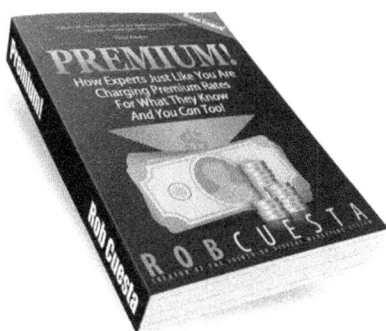

Follow-up sequence

Of course, the whole point of this exercise is to follow-up, so you'll need a follow-up email sequence, which we'll create in the next chapter.

Your Amazon listing

It would also be very useful if you have an Amazon listing that actually converts—in other words, when someone finds a book on Amazon they're likely to buy—and some reviews on the Amazon page, because that gives you the social proof that makes people want to buy the book even if they've never heard of it or you.

Multiple Bonuses vs. a Single Bonus

One question that I get asked by clients is whether you really need multiple bonuses, or you can just offer a single bonus for the whole book.

First, remember that there's a simple trade off here: the more you offer, the more likely it is that someone will sign up for the bonuses.

Now, that's not just about value. Yes, if you offer three bonuses, they have more perceived value than if you just offered one.

More importantly, however, it gives you the opportunity to deliver your content in multiple formats. Different people learn—and like to consume information—in different ways. Some people want to watch videos, others want to read. Some people want to listen to audio, and some just want to read a few bullet points. Some people want a picture they can take in with a single glance on their screen, others want something they can hold in their hands.

If all you've got is a video, then a large proportion of your audience isn't getting what they want, and they may decide they don't want your bonus at all.

If you have a set of video chapter summaries, you can turn those into MP3s as well, and get a designer to create an infographic of your main diagnostic process (if you have one). Finally, create a checklist that the reader can print out and complete. Now you've addressed the needs and preferences of your entire audience, and everyone will find something valuable in that bonus stack that they want to get.

It's not about creating new content. It's about taking content that's already in the book and presenting it in different formats for people to consume.

Also, remember that "one vs. many" can also come down to how you package things. If you have eight chapters, each with a worksheet, you can either present it as a single bonus of a set of worksheets or as eight separate bonuses. It's all in the wording you use in your call to action.

11

Reader Bonus Step 1

The first step of the Reader Bonus funnel is to get people to opt in. Here are some examples of good lead-capture pages.

Please note, these are not my clients; they are well-known, successful experts who have a good optin page.

The first is for Michael Gerber's book *Beyond the E-Myth*.

It's a very clean, simple page. "Simply enter your details be-low and we'll email you the download links and further details for multi-purchase bonuses. Click here to see the bonuses." Even though the reader has come from the book, so they should know what the bonuses are, don't assume they'll remember. You want as many peoples as possible to opt in, so reminding them of the bonuses is a good idea.

Then it continues. "Still need to order the book? Visit Ama-zon here or for bulk hardcover purchases, please contact us." Again, remember that people might reach this page from a web search, not necessarily from the book, so it's a good idea to have a link to Amazon for people who haven't bought the book yet.

The interesting thing about this form is the two fields on the right for the reader to enter their Amazon order number, the date of purchase, and how many copies they bought.

As far as the number of copies purchased goes, Gerber was offering a range of bonuses for multi-copy orders, so he may have had a member of his team reviewing each optin and com-paring it to sales reports to check it was valid.

The Amazon order number, though, is something else. As a publisher, you don't have access to your buyers' order num-bers. So, the team member can't check the numbers themselves. Instead, they may simply be checking that the number looks valid. The more likely explanation, however, is that the field is there simply to discourage people from trying their luck.

Personally, I'm torn over whether to include that question or not. Usually, I discourage my clients from making it harder for people to opt in. After all, if someone wants your bonuses — even if they haven't got your book — they are interested in what you do, and you have the opportunity to start a conversation with them. So, it's up to you whether you want to add an "order number" field and have fewer optins, or leave it out and maximize your list size. It's also up to you whether you check what people enter in that field!

The next example is for Brendon Burchard's book *High Performance Habits*.

Again, he tells you what his bonuses are going to be. I particularly like the second bonus, a free Professional Performance

Assessment. Quizzes and assessments are great bonuses for books.

Like Gerber, he's asking people to enter their Amazon receipt number as a "gatekeeper" to reduce the number of non-readers who ask for the bonuses.

I've also seen authors use content from the book as a test question, for example "Enter the first word of Chapter 5." That's a question you can actually check the answer to, so if you're determined to only give the bonus to real readers, it's a better way to go. If you do decide to go this way, make the question one that can be answered in any format, including ebooks: ebooks don't have page numbers, so don't ask "the fifth word on page 87."

Here's a simpler page for *Get Rich Lucky Bitch*.

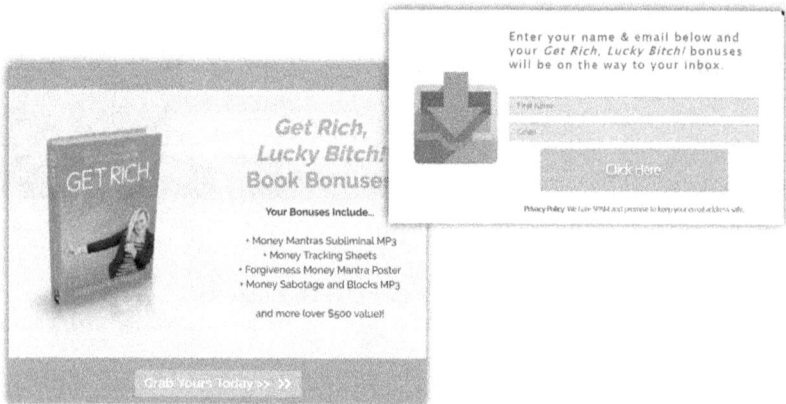

This time there's no verification question.

One point to note is that the optin form is a popup, making this what's called a 2-step optin.

Putting the form on a popup like this can often increase optin rates. When the form is displayed on the main page, the visitor has to decide whether the bonuses are worth surrendering their privacy. With the button and popup, the visitor doesn't even know there's a form to fill in, so the initial question is simply whether they want the bonuses.

At this point, a principle called commitment and consistency (discussed in Robert Cialdini's book *Influence*) kicks in: the visitor has already taken a simple step that indicates they are interested in the bonuses, so it's much easier to get them to take the next step. Also, if they didn't fill in their details now, it would be at odds with the decision they made a moment earlier to click the button.

The next example shows a clever way to get the visitor to qualify themselves. It's the optin page for Scott Fox's *Click Millionaires*.

In order to claim the free bonuses, you have to "complete the short reader survey." That creates a great opportunity to find out what kind of people are buying your book, but also allows you to ask questions to gauge how suitable your solution is for them.

What I love about this is that, even if someone hasn't bought your book, you're going to get value from them.

12

Sign up for ClickFunnels for just $19/month

PLEASE NOTE: Everything in this chapter is correct as I write this. However, I have no relationship to ClickFunnels—except as a devoted user, fan, and affiliate—so I can't say whether the offer will still exist six months from now or even six days from now. If it's not there, take heart: even at $97, ClickFunnels is such a powerful system, and it will help your business so much, that it's well worth the investment.

In any case, you'll have a 14-day free trial, so if you just want to try it out and set up the funnels in this book, be my guest!

Before you start to build your funnel, you're going to need an account with ClickFunnels.

If you have ClickFunnels already, that's great. If not, I can show you how to get access to the system at a very reduced rate.

Normally ClickFunnels is $97 or $297 a month. However, as a reader of this book, I'm going to show you how you can get it for just $19 a month.

On this plan, you'll have access to the full functionality of the $97 plan, but with some restrictions:

1) You can only use funnels that are "shared" with you — you can't create them from scratch. That's not a problem, because I'm going to share the funnels you need for this book.

2) You're restricted to just 3 funnels. That's not a problem because by the time you need more funnels you should be generating money from your existing funnels.

3) You're restricted to 10 pages. That's not a problem because I've made sure you don't need more than that for the funnels I'm sharing with you.

4) You'll need to sign up with an email address that isn't already on ClickFunnels' mailing list

---

Visit this URL to import your first funnel:

www.brightflamebooks.com/bonusshare

(Note, you may have to type the address into your browser)

This is a special plan that's not available by signing up at ClickFunnels.com. When you're ready to move up, you'll be able to upgrade to the $97 plan easily, but you can stay on the $19 plan for as long as you need.

If you're already a ClickFunnels customer, don't worry: you'll be able to import the funnels for this book into your account and work with them just like the funnels you create yourself, and with no restrictions ☺

13

Importing Your Funnel

If you haven't imported your funnel yet, you'll need to do that first.

To Import Your Funnel

Go to http://brightflamebooks.com/bonusshare
to import the Reader Bonus funnel
(you may have to type the address into your browser).

NB: If you imported the funnel earlier, you don't need to import it again.

You'll be taken to a landing page with an introductory video and an overview of the funnel.

If you're a new user, enter your email address and a password. If you've opted in for an offer (book, webinar, etc.) from Click-Funnels in the past, use a different email if you can, otherwise you may not be offered the $19 plan on the next page.

If you're an existing ClickFunnels user, you can login at the top right corner and import the funnel into your account.

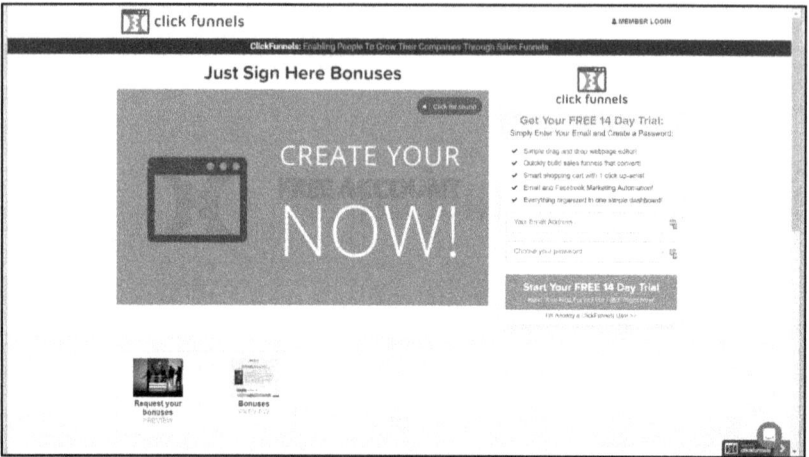

On the next page, you can select the plan that's right for you.

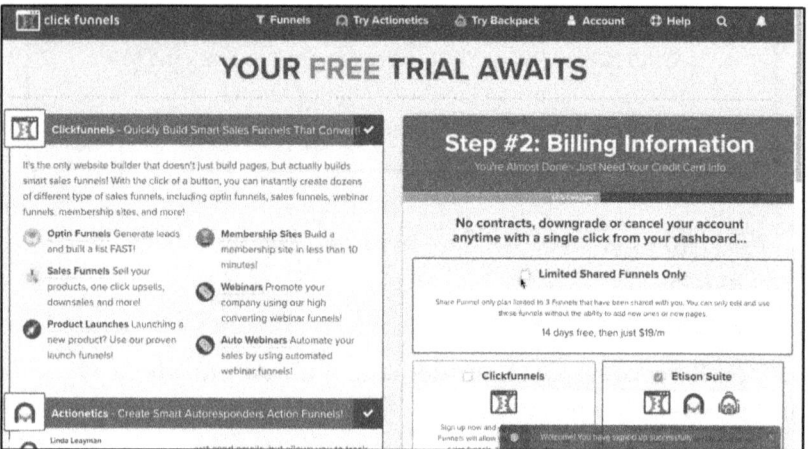

14

Integrate ClickFunnels and ActiveCampaign

If you've made it this far, you have a working ActiveCampaign account and a working ClickFunnels account. In order to build your funnels, you'll need to get the two of them to talk to each other. First, go into ActiveCampaign and click on your name in the top right corner, then click on <Settings>. In the list of options on the left, click on <Developer>

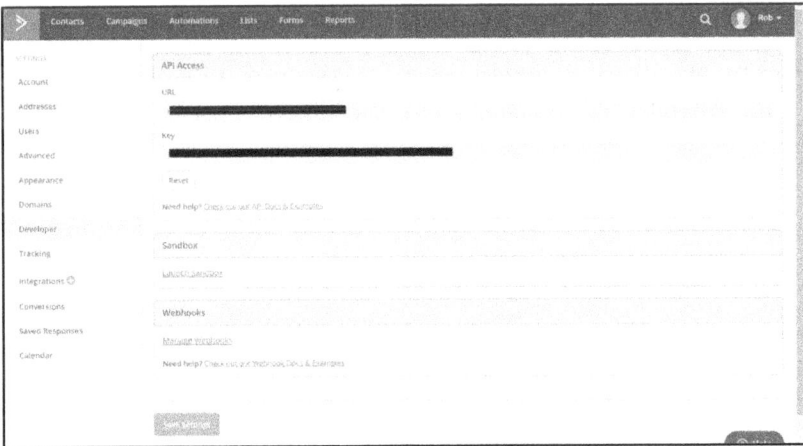

The information we need is in the two boxes labelled "URL" and "Key", and I suggest you copy and paste them into a notepad document.

Next go back to ClickFunnels, and along the top click on <Account> and then <Integrations>.

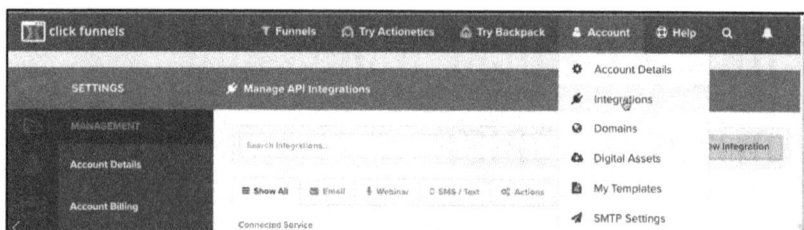

Next, click [Add new integration]

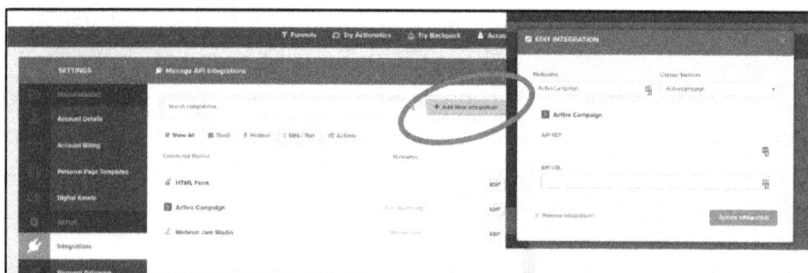

Enter ActiveCampaign as a nickname, choose ActiveCampaign from the list of services on the right.

Next, enter the ActiveCampaign API Key and URL you copied earlier.

ATTENTION: ClickFunnels asks for these in the opposite order to how they are shown in ActiveCampaign, so make sure you put the right code into each box.

Click [Update Integration] and you're all set.

15

Managing File Assets

If you are giving people free downloads as a thank you for buying your book, you need somewhere online to store those files.

> Note: You only have to do this for files the user will <u>download</u> to their own computer, like reports, worksheets, infographics, etc. Don't worry about uploading media files like videos.

Managing small download files (Under 3Mb)

If your files are under 3Mb and are in one of the supported file types (jpg, jpeg, gif, png, pdf, zip, txt, csv, or xls), you can upload them directly into ClickFunnels.

To store a file in ClickFunnels, click on <Account> on the top menu bar, then click on <Digital Assets>.

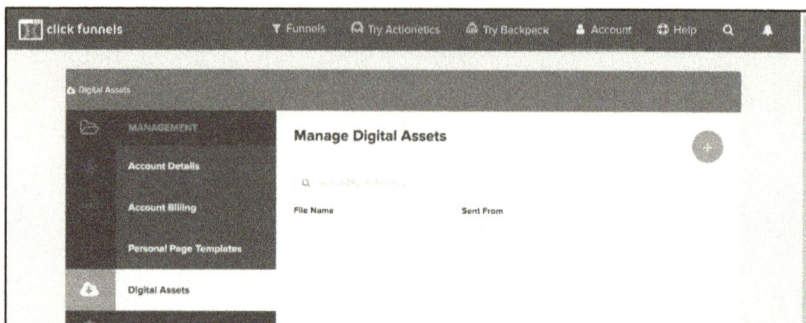

Initially, the list is empty, so to add your first file, click on the green circle with a cross in the upper right-hand corner.

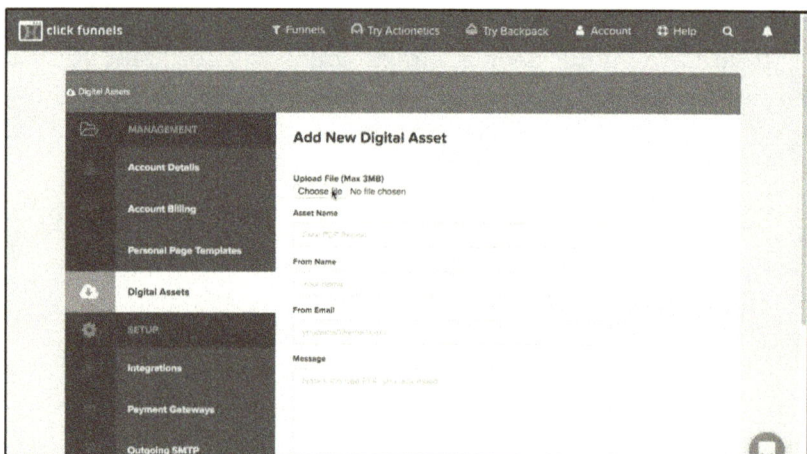

1) Click on [Choose File] and select the file you want to upload from your computer.
2) Give the asset a meaningful name, so that you'll be able to recognize it later in the list of assets.
3) Scroll down to the bottom of the page and click [Add]

You can ignore the other boxes — they are used by ClickFunnels' own email management system, Actionetics. As we are using ActiveCampaign, you don't need to fill those fields in.

Recording the asset URLs

ClickFunnels will take you out to the Manage Digital Assets page, which now shows your newly uploaded file.

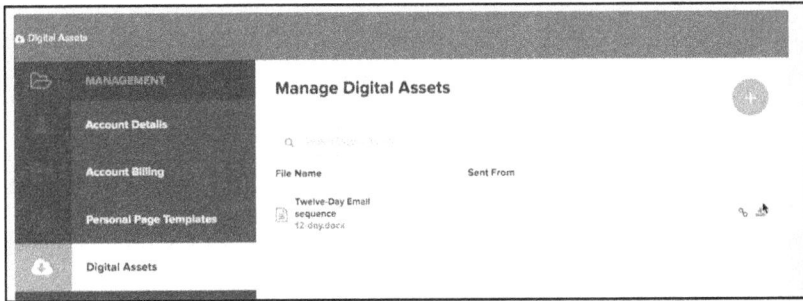

Later, when you're editing your funnel, you'll need to know the URL of the file. The problem is, it's hard to get back to this screen from the editor, so a useful tip here is to open a new Word file or a text file in Notepad (or whatever the equivalent is for your computer) and paste the link into it. To do that, click on the chain-link symbol to the right of your file name. That will automatically copy the link to your clipboard and you can paste it directly into your text document for later

For files over 3Mb, or unsupported formats, you'll need some third-party cloud storage (a service that stores your files online rather than on your own computer). Avoid services like Dropbox or OneDrive: those files are also stored on your computer and it's very easy to forget what they are and delete, move, or rename them. It's safer to use a dedicated solution like Amazon's AWS (Amazon Web Server).

Exercise

Upload any files that users will be downloading as bonuses.

16

Customizing your Optin Page

Phew! We are FINALLY ready to work on your first funnel.

It's taken a while to get here, but a lot of what we have done is one-off setup, and you've also learned a lot of new skills to get to this point.

So, we are going to start by customizing the first page of your new funnel to make it your own.

What we are going to look at in this chapter is

- Changing an image
- Uploading your own images
- Changing the background image
- Editing the text
- Changing the copyright notice

The first page is simple: just a sign-up form, a picture of the book, a background image, and some text.

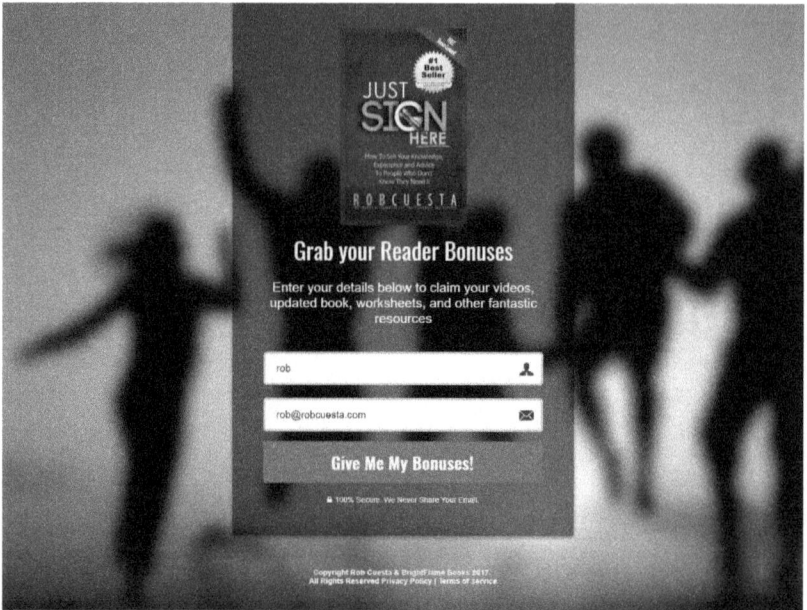

Opening a funnel

In the top menu of ClickFunnels, click <Funnels> and then <Browse Funnels>. This will bring you to a page that lists all the funnels active in your system—which for now should be just one.

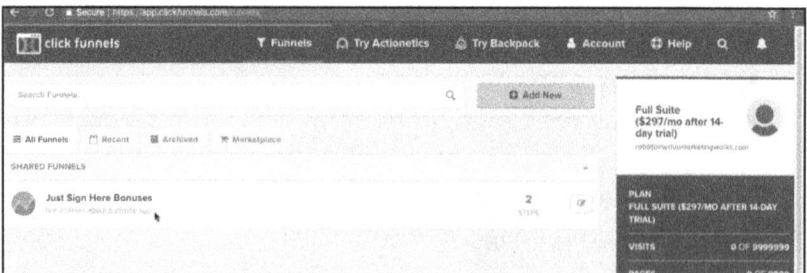

Click on the name of the funnel you want to edit, and it will take you into the main funnel overview page.

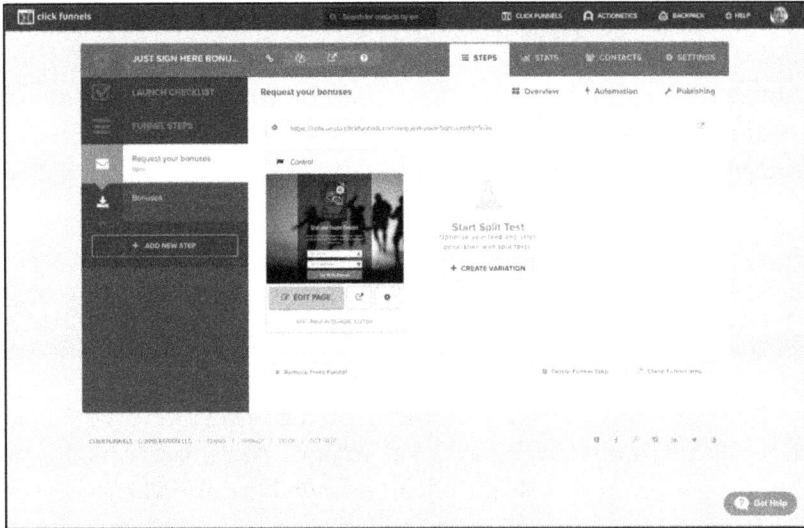

Down the left-hand side of the screen is a list of all the pages in the funnel. Each page corresponds to a step, so in this funnel there are two steps: the Optin page and the Thank you page.

On the right of the screen, you can see a thumbnail of the currently selected page – you can change that by clicking on the name of a page in the left column.

You also have the option to create a second version of the page if you wanted to do split testing.

Split testing is a technical term for running two different versions of a page side by side, so you can see which performs better. When you set up a split test in ClickFunnels, the system will select which of the alternative versions to display to visitors at random, and then track how many people took action on each version. Any time you make a substantial change to the design or content of a page in a funnel, I recommend you split test it against the original. That way, you'll know whether the changes have improved your conversion rate or harmed it.

By default, when you open a funnel to edit it, ClickFunnels will show you information about the first page in the funnel. To edit the contents of a page, first click its name in the left-hand column, so that it is highlighted, then click the [EDIT PAGE] button below the thumbnail.

Switching the Book Cover

To swap the book cover for a picture of your own book, move your mouse over the cover image. You'll see a blue border appear around it, and then an orange border. When you see the orange border, click on it and a new panel will open on the right of the screen (If you click the image again, the panel will disappear, and you can bring it back by clicking on the cover image again).

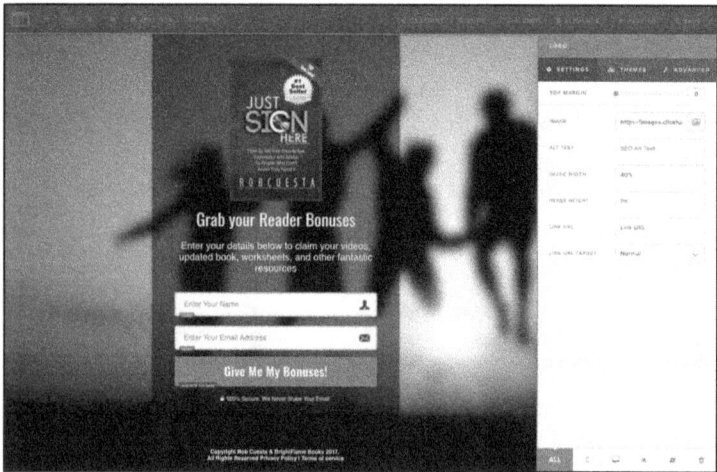

The main panel shows 7 settings:

Top Margin: This slider allows you to add blank space above your image.

Image: This is the reference to the image file you want to use

Alt Text: This is the text that is displayed in a browser when the picture is still downloading. It's also used for accessibility, so it's a good idea to change it to something meaningful.

Image Width and Height: These boxes control the size of the image on screen. If you leave the boxes blank, ClickFunnels will try to display the image at full size, or scale it down to fit if the image is larger than the available space. If you enter numeric values, ClickFunnels will scale the image to that size. Finally, if you enter a percentage in the width box and leave the other empty, ClickFunnels will scale the image to use that proportion of the space available. In the image above, for example, Image Width is set to 40%, so the image has been scaled to take up 40% of the available width. Cleverly, if you leave one of the boxes blank, ClickFunnels will scale the image but maintain the aspect ratio, whichever of the 3 methods you used. To get used to what different options do, change the values in these two boxes and see what happens to the image in the preview — just remember to set it back to Width 50%, Height blank afterwards!

Link URL: If you put a URL in here, ClickFunnels will open that page when a viewer clicks the image.

Link URL Target: If you've specified a Link URL, you can tell ClickFunnels whether the page should be opened in the current window or it should open a new tab or window to display the page.

For our purposes, the only options we need to edit are the IMAGE value and the width.

Picking a new cover image

To display the cover of your own book, click the mountain icon to the right of the IMAGE box.

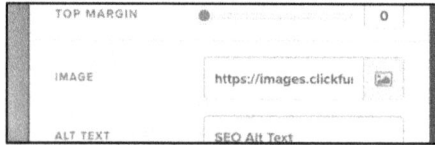

This displays a browser of all the images you already have uploaded in your system. At this stage, if you've just created your account, your list will be blank—the current images for this funnel are actually sitting in my account because the funnel was shared from there.

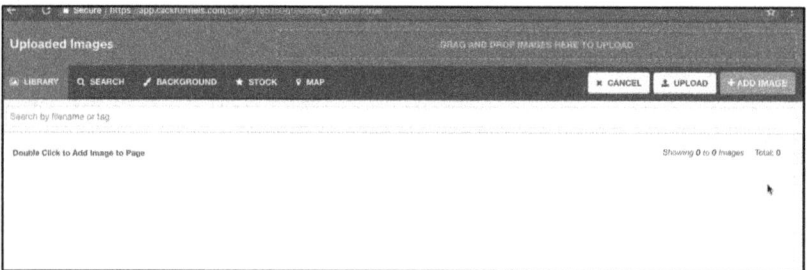

To add your own image, you'll first need to upload it, so click the [UPLOAD] button and browse to the file you want to use. When the file finishes uploading, it will appear in the image browser. Click on it to highlight it, then click the green [+ ADD IMAGE] button. You'll see that your new image is now displayed.

Changing the Background

Switching the background image is very similar. However, the background setting is hidden away — you can't just click on the background and change it.

Click on <SETTINGS> in the top bar and a sub-menu will appear.

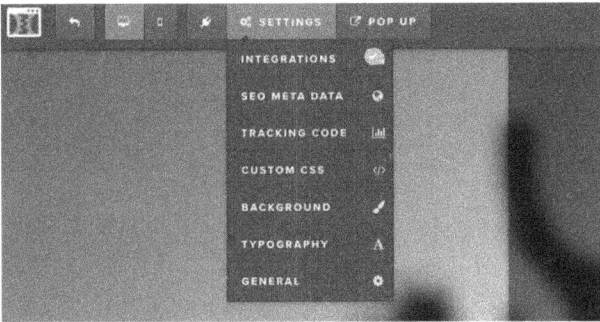

Click on <BACKGROUND> and a new panel will appear on the right of the screen.

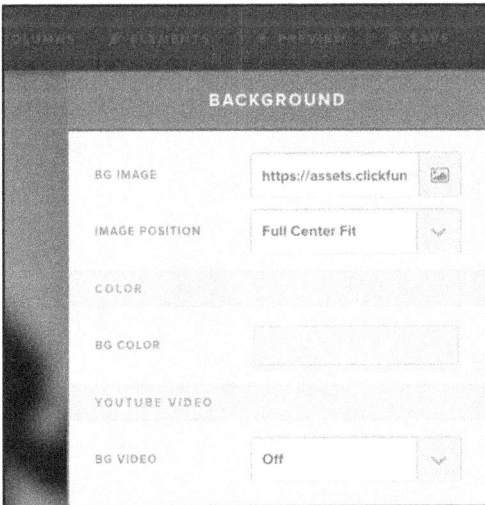

To change the background image, click the mountain icon next to the BG IMAGE box, which will open your image browser again.

If you have an image you want to use, you can upload it and add it just as we did with the book cover.

However, there are a couple of other options available to you.

First, ClickFunnels has some simple backgrounds built in that you can choose from. Click <BACKGROUND> to see them.

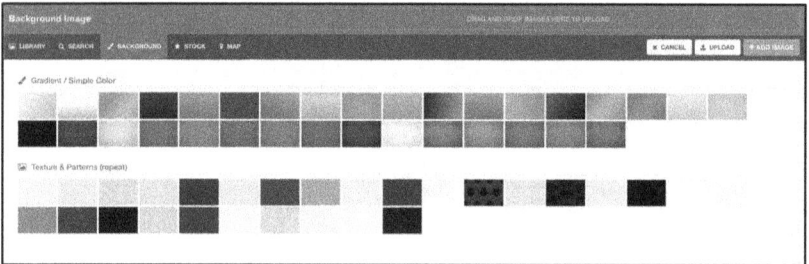

Alternatively, if you click the box next to BG COLOR, you can set a solid color as the background to the page. (You'll need to delete the Image URL in order for the color to be shown).

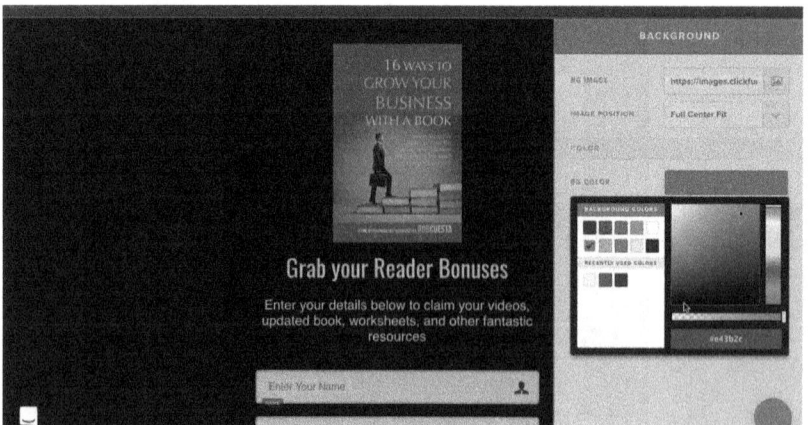

Finally, if you're feeling adventurous, you can use a YouTube video as your page background by setting BG VIDEO to On.

For now, pick one of the stock backgrounds or a solid color.

Editing the Text

Editing text in ClickFunnels is simple. Click on the text you want to edit and make any changes you want to the wording. The key point to notice is that the Heading and the text are in separate   boxes.

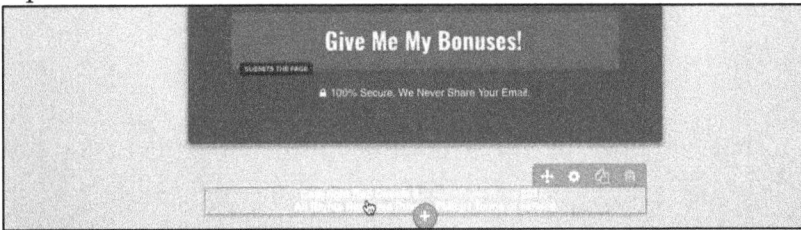

The copyright text at the bottom of the page is edited in the same way. Depending on what background color you've set, you may not be able to see it now(!), but it is there. Hover your mouse over the copyright text until the orange border appears.

Click on the cogwheel (the second icon in the icon bar) to access the settings for this text box: you'll be able to change the appearance of your text—font, text size, color—along with other settings.

Editing hyperlinks

When you change the text color, you'll notice that the color of the words "BrightFlame Books" stays the same. That's because these words are hyperlinked—it's the same problem you get in Microsoft Word and other word processors: when you change the text of a paragraph, it doesn't affect the color of hyperlinks.

To change that in ClickFunnels, you need to edit the hyperlink itself. Click on the hyperlinked text and a small blue icon of a pencil in a square will appear at the left end of the text.

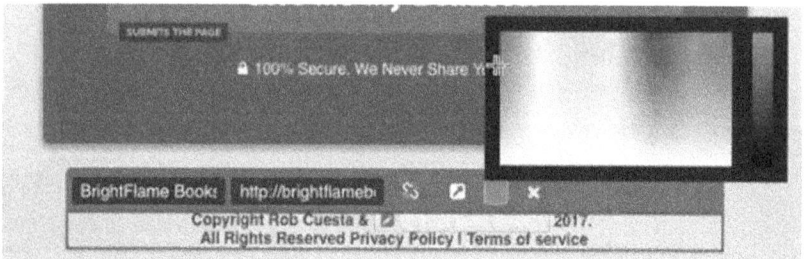

Reading along the icon bar you have:

1. **The linked text.** This is what will be displayed on the page. To change this, click in the box, delete the existing content and replace.

2. **The linked URL.** This is the page the viewer is sent to if they click the link. Again, to change this, click in the box, delete the existing URL and replace.

3. **Unlink.** Click this icon to remove the hyperlink.

4. **Open in.** Click this icon to choose whether the link will open in a new window/tab or the existing window.

5. **Link color.** Click the color swatch to open a color picker which will allow you to set the color of the hyperlink text

6. **Close.** Click this to close the link settings panel.

Exercise

Change the front page of the funnel to be about your book. Update the cover, the text, and the footer.

17

Linking Your Funnel to ActiveCampaign

Now that our funnel looks how we want it, it's time to connect it to Active Campaign so that anyone who opts in is added to our mailing list.

The integration settings for individual pages are up in the page settings menu (where we found the background settings before). Click on <SETTINGS> in the top bar and the sub-menu will appear again. <INTEGRATIONS> is the first item.

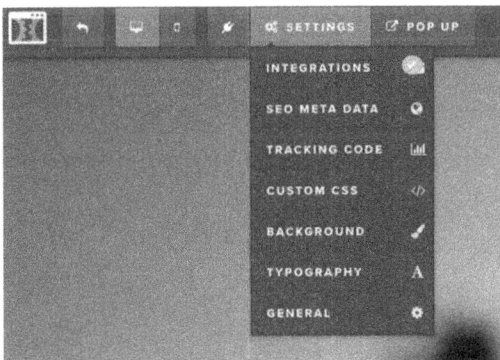

That will bring up a panel with options for what happens when someone fills in the optin form.

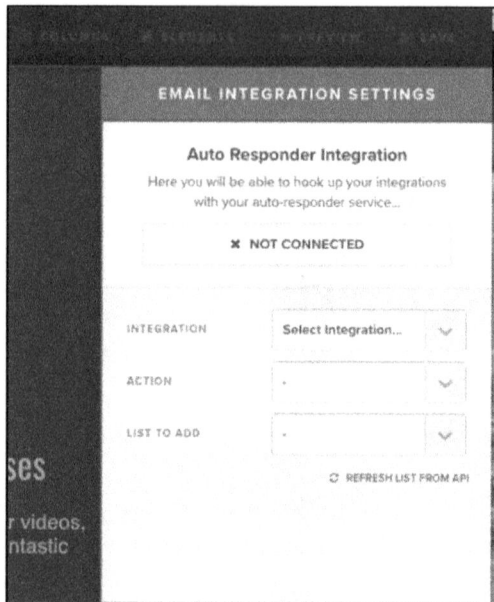

To connect ActiveCampaign, click where it says "Select Integration..." and pick ActiveCampaign from the dropdown menu.

In the next box, ACTION, select "Add to list" and in the "LIST TO ADD" box, pick your Reader Bonus list. If the list isn't shown, click just below that, where it says "REFRESH LIST FROM API" to force ActiveCampaign to fetch information from ActiveCampaign.

When you're done, click anywhere outside the settings pane to close it.

Other Settings

Before we leave our page, there are a couple more settings we may want to look at.

General Settings

First, there's a set of general settings for the page. Again, click <SETTINGS> in the top bar, and pick the final item <GENERAL>.

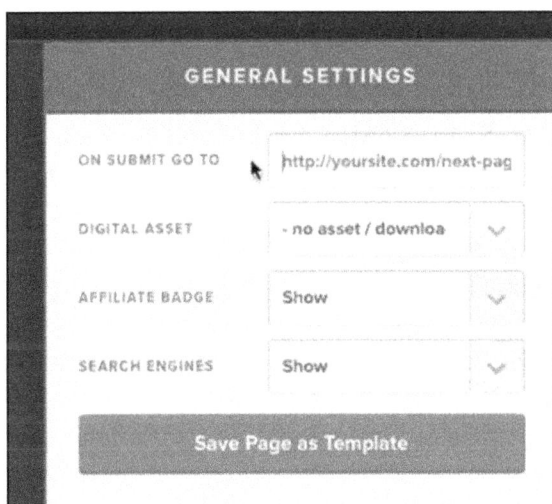

ON SUBMIT GO TO: By default, when someone fills in the optin form and submits, ClickFunnels takes them to the next page in the funnel. If you want to send them somewhere else — a page on your website, for example — you can put a URL in this box. For this exercise, you can leave it blank because we want ClickFunnels to take the visitor to the next page.

DIGITAL ASSET: Ignore this for now.

AFFILIATE BADGE: Every ClickFunnels user is automatically also an affiliate. This option adds a small button at the bottom of your page. If someone clicks it, they'll go to a ClickFunnels sales page, and if they sign up you get paid. That's great, but on optin pages we only want one thing for visitors to do, so I suggest you turn this off for this page (you can turn it on for the second page, after you've got their email address!).

SEARCH ENGINES: If this is turned off, search engines like Google and Bing won't be able to see the page, so it won't turn up in searches. Whether you have this on or off comes back to the debate earlier about whether you want to allow non-readers to opt in. If you don't, turn this off. If you're happy for non-readers to find your page and add themselves to your list, turn it on.

SAVE PAGE AS TEMPLATE: Don't be fooled by the fact that this looks like a save button for this panel. What this button does is save the current page as a template that you can use when creating pages in your own funnels. So, at this stage, DON'T CLICK IT!

To close the settings panel, click anywhere on the page outside the panel.

SEO META DATA

The final set of options you need to set — and ClickFunnels will stop you from saving a new page if you haven't set these — is the SEO Metadata options.

These control what is shown in search engines, at the top of the browser window, and if someone shares your optin page on social media. So, they're pretty important!

Again, click on <SETTINGS> at the top, and then <SEO METADATA>. A new options panel will open on the right of the screen.

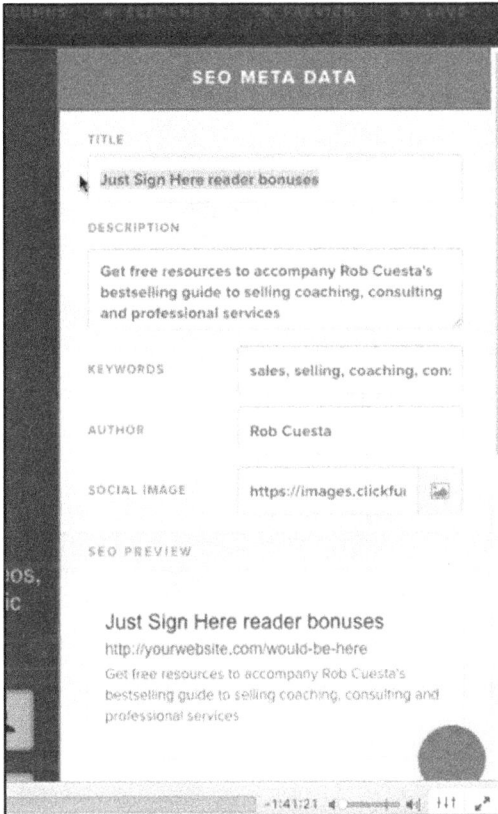

Right now, everything is set to the metadata for my book *Just Sign Here*, so you'll want to change it to be about your book. You can see what search engines see in the "SEO PREVIEW" window.

TITLE: This is the title of the page (not the book!). It will show up at the top of the browser window, and also as the heading in search engines.

DESCRIPTION: This is the text that will show up in search engines. It's also what Facebook will show by default when someone types the page URL in a post.

KEYWORDS: If you're allowing search engines to see the page, add keywords here that will help your page to be found.

AUTHOR: Enter your name or your company's. "Authorship" used to be a "thing" in Google. It isn't any more, so this field is redundant for now. However, Google is a fickle master and it may come back one day, so you may as well set it and forget it.

SOCIAL IMAGE: This is the image that will be displayed in Facebook posts, etc. Set it the same way as any other image in ClickFunnels. If you're going to use your cover as the social image and you uploaded it in the earlier step, you don't need to upload it again. It's already in your image browser, so you can simply click on it to highlight it, then click [ADD IMAGE].

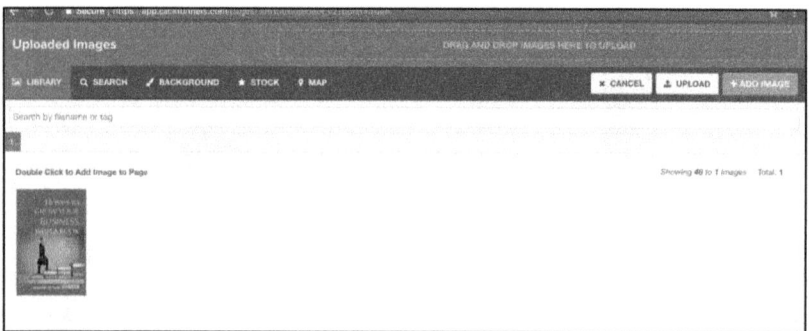

Saving your work

Once your page looks how you want it, all that's left is to save your work. This is important: ClickFunnels doesn't save your changes as you go along — you need to click save.

The [SAVE] button is at the top of the page, on the right.

Next to it, you'll see a [PREVIEW] button. This will open your page in a new window in view mode (rather than edit mode, which is what you're currently looking at). Now, I'm a huge fan of ClickFunnels, as you've probably figured out. The Preview button is one thing that I think they got completely wrong. Why do I say that? Because you have to save your changes for them to be reflected in the preview. So, it's really a View function rather than a Preview. On the scale of things, though, it's a minor point, and one that I can live with given that the editor shows you the effect of your changes as you go.

Once you've saved, you can hit the Exit button, which is at the top, on the left, next to the ClickFunnels icon. Again, this is an odd one. It uses a left arrow, which means "undo" in most editors. Luckily, if you accidentally hit it without saving, ClickFunnels will pop up a warning.

18

The Bonus Delivery Page

Now that the optin page is connected, our next task is to update the second page, where subscribers get to download their bonuses. You can give your readers as many or as few bonuses as you like—the one in the sample funnel has slots for many bonuses in case you want to offer a resource for most chapters.

To get to the second page, once you exit the optin page and you are back at the funnel overview, click on its name ("Bonuses") in the pane on the left.

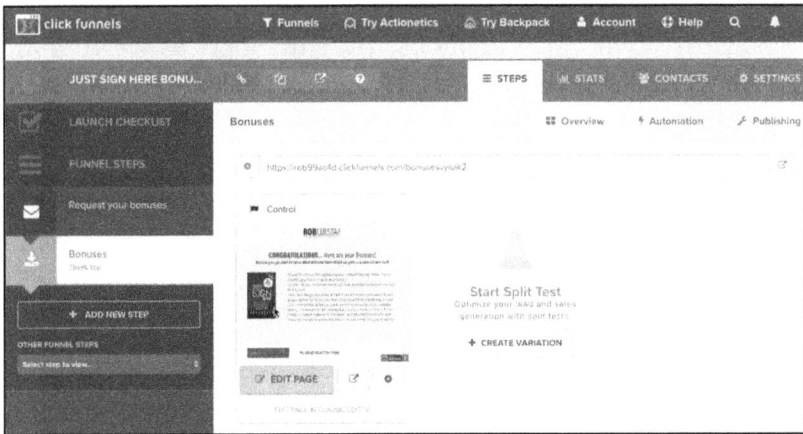

You'll see the name of the page in the title bar change, and the thumbnail will be updated. When you're ready, click [EDIT PAGE] and you'll go into the editor.

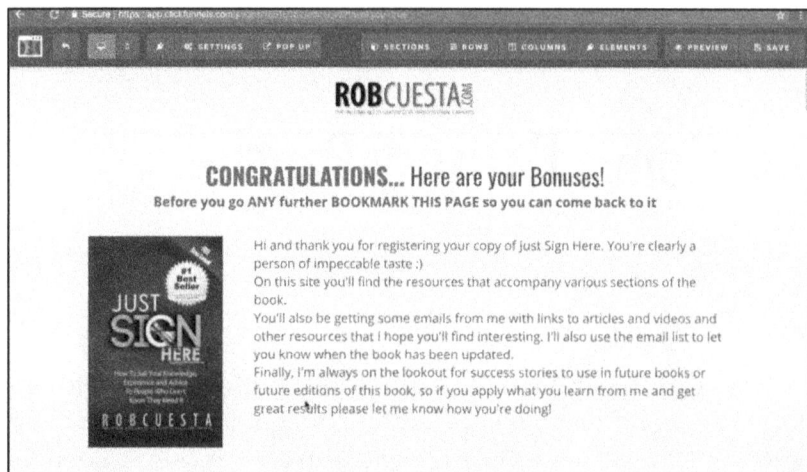

Updating the Logo

First, let's change the logo at the top of the page.

Start by hovering your mouse over the logo, as we've done for other items we want to change, and when the orange border appears, click the image.

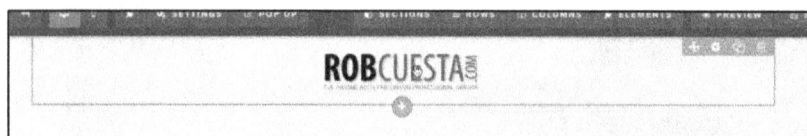

That will open up the image options page that we've seen several times now, and you can upload a new image and add it to the page—it's exactly the same as updating the book cover on the optin page.

A note on Image settings

Just as with the cover image earlier, we can add a margin at the top, set alt text, set width and height, and turn the image into a clickable link by adding a Link URL.

Most of the time, if we set a specific dimension for an image, it's the width, so that we can get it to fit into a column of text. In the case of logos, however, we're far more likely to specify height. A good height for logos is 60px, because we don't want them to take up too much space on screen and push more important elements "below the fold."

ABOVE AND BELOW THE FOLD: You'll hear designers and marketers talk about things being above or below "the fold". This is a term borrowed from print media, in particular newspapers and magazines. It comes from the habit of displaying newspapers in piles, folded in half, so that browsers only typically see what's in the top half of the cover (above the fold). They'll only see stuff below the fold if they pick the paper up and start reading. So, if you have something important and you want to be sure people will see it, it needs to be above the fold.

Something very similar happens on web pages: a visitor typically only looks at what's on screen when they first arrive on your page. Once they've seen that, they'll make up their mind whether they want to bother scrolling down to the rest of the page.

So, web designers refer to the area of the page corresponding to that opening screen as "above the fold" and anything that can't be seen until you scroll down as "below the fold." And, just like a newspaper editor, you want to be sure that you get your critical content above the fold, so visitors will see it as soon as they arrive.

Keeping logos small gives you more room for that important content, so I typically set logos to just 60 pixels high.

Advanced Image options

On the settings pane, if you click <ADVANCED> over on the right, it will offer additional options.

ALIGN: Display the image on the left, right, or in the middle of the available space.

RADIUS: Round off the image corners.

BORDER: Show a border around the edges of the image.

SHADOW: Show a drop shadow behind the image.

OPACITY: Make the image semi-transparent so you can see the background through it.

GREY SCALE FX: Show a grey-scale version of the image.

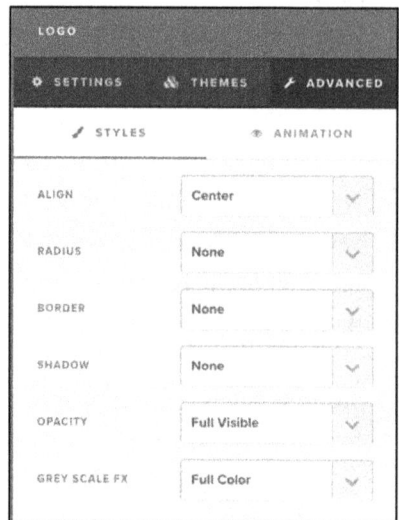

Updating the content

If you've been following along with the exercise so far, you already have the skills you need to

- Make changes to headlines and text (page 131 "Editing the Text")
- Swap out the images (page 126 "Switching the Book Cover")
- Update weblinks (page 132 "Editing hyperlinks")

So, I won't repeat those here.

Video Settings

The video on the page is one that I bought on Fiverr.com that simply asks people to leave a review of the book. You can get your own version with your own words (for example you might want to change the style of the video or add the link to your Amazon page at the end) very cheaply.

To change the video, as you can probably guess, click the video in the editor and it will bring up a set of options on the right. Most of them are fairly self-explanatory.

VIDEO TYPE: ClickFunnels accepts videos hosted on a range of popular platforms, not just YouTube.

URL: Depending on the "type" you select above, this box will change to allow you to tell ClickFunnels where the video is. For YouTube, it's simply the URL of the page for that video. However, it must be the full www.youtube.com/ link. If you have a link that looks like www.youtu.be/..., paste it into a browser first; it will redirect to the link you need and you can copy it from there. Also, if the link has an "&" followed by more text, delete the "&" and everything after it. **If you don't use the correct link in the correct format, the video won't play on your ClickFunnels page.**

✓ https://www.youtube.com/watch?v=WUUbygMzhRA

✗ https://youtu.be/WUUbygMzhRA

✗ https://www.youtube.com/watch?v=WUUbygMzhRA&feature=youtu.be

AUTOPLAY: Some people hate videos that play automatically (especially if they're working in an open office and they don't have headphones!), many site owners love them. Beware, though, that Chrome now prevents many videos from playing automatically, regardless of what you pick here! Also, autoplay is blocked on mobile devices.

CONTROLS: Displays or hides the bar at the bottom of the video with the play/pause icon, timeline, etc.

BRANDING: Hides the hosting logo unless the mouse is hovering over the video.

BLOCK PAUSE: As the name suggests, this will prevent the user from pausing your video. That's great for evergreen webinars, where you want to maintain the illusion that they're watching a live video. For this page, though, you can leave this set to NO.

OPTIONAL WIDTH/HEIGHT: Allow you to specify the size of the video on screen. If

OVERLAY TEXT: If you set block pause to on, this allows you to display a text overlay when the user first opens the page.

Advanced Video Options

On the Advanced tab in the options panel, you'll find three additional settings.

WIDTH: Allows you to quickly set how much of the available column the video will take up (full width, ¾ or ½).

STICKY ON SCROLL: If you set this on, as a user scrolls down the page, the video will float down so it stays visible.

PADDING: Allows you to add space around your video.

The Review Button

You can update the link on this button to point to your book's page on Amazon. Alternatively, you can create a custom link specifically to leave a review by replacing the X's in the following link with your book's ASIN (Amazon's product code, not your ISBN):

https://www.amazon.com/review/create-
review?asin=XXXXXX

The [WATCH] Button Video Popup

The black [WATCH] button opens up a popup with a video that tells people how to leave a review on Amazon (never assume people know how to do even the most basic tasks!). You are welcome to leave that video, or replace it with your own.

THUMBNAIL URL: Allows you to specify an image to be shown on the page. Currently this is set to a black button, which is a simple way to create a graphical button.

VIDEO URL: As before, this is the location where your video is hosted.

ALT TEXT: Alternative text for the thumbnail image.

THUMBNAIL WIDTH AND HEIGHT: Controls the size at of the button on screen

The **advanced** options for a video popup are the same as for a normal video, as above.

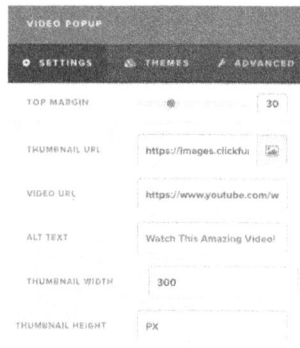

The Resource download buttons

As you scroll down the page, you'll see many sections with different bonuses. Each section has a button linked to where the relevant file is stored. Some of the buttons, e.g. the [Buy on Amazon] buttons in Step 5, are images with a hyperlink, which you can edit exactly as we did earlier. The [Download] buttons, however, use functionality built into ClickFunnels to create a simple text button. Here's how to edit them.

Changing the file

Let's change Step 2. At the moment, it's pointing to the latest version of my book, but let's use the file you uploaded earlier in Managing File Assets.

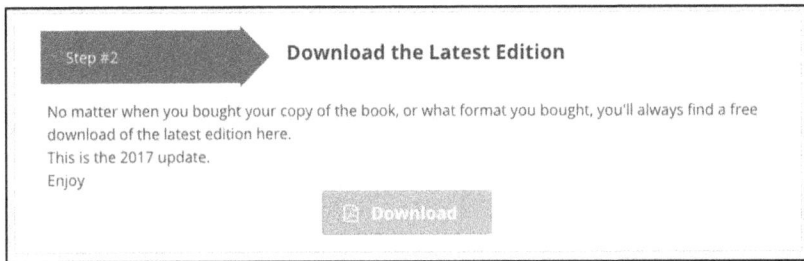

Start by editing the text to say "Download…" and whatever your bonus is. Then change the text below that to a description of what they'll be downloading.

Finally, let's update the button. Start, as always, by clicking the button so the options pane opens on the right.

EDIT ACTION: This allows you to select what will happen when someone clicks the button.

- **SUBMIT ORDER/FORM:** If there is a form on the page, the button will send the in-

formation in the form to whatever app is linked to it (e.g. ActiveCampaign). N.B. This page doesn't have a form, so it's not relevant here.

- **OPEN THE POPUP:** ClickFunnels allows you to create a popup window — useful, as I said earlier, for two-step optins. This option opens the popup when the button is clicked.

- **GO TO URL:** This is the option we are using here. You can link to a page or to a file stored somewhere in the cloud. You can also tell ClickFunnels whether to open the file in the same window or open a new tab/window for it — for files, a new window is always best, as you don't want to take people away from your site.

- **GO TO NEXT STEP:** This will simply take the visitor to the next page in the funnel without submitting a form.

- **SCROLL TO ROW/SECTION:** You can select any row or section on the page and the window will scroll to that specific part of the page when the button is clicked.

- **SHOW/HIDE ACTION:** Use this to show or hide part of the page when the button is clicked.

BUTTON TEXT: To change the text displayed on the button, change what's in this box.

SUB TEXT: To display a second line of text in a smaller font, type the text in here.

FONT FAMILY/SIZE/SUBTEXT SIZE: Use these two options to change how the button text and sub text are displayed.

MOBILE SIZE/MOBILE SUB SIZE: For mobile devices, you'll probably want to display the text in a smaller font. Use these two sliders to set those sizes.

TEXT COLOR: Opens a color picker so you can change the color of the text.

BG COLOR: Opens a color picker to change the background color of the button.

Advanced Settings

If you click the [ADVANCED] tab, you'll see many options for controlling how your button is displayed. The only one you need to worry about for now is ICON PICKER. This will allow you to change the icon displayed to the left of the text on the button—it's currently set to a PDF file icon.

Setting the file destination

As I said, we are using the "GO TO URL" option for this page, so let's point this to the file you uploaded earlier. Back in *Managing File Assets*, you pasted the link to your bonus file into a text document. Go back to that file now, copy the URL, and paste it into the GOTO URL field. If your file is hosted somewhere else (because it's too large or not a supported type) you can use its URL here instead.

When you're done, click [BACK] on this settings pane to take you to the main options, or click anywhere on the page to exit the settings.

Editing the layout

Let's say you don't have a few hundred bonuses, like I do for this book (just kidding—as you can see, there's only 97!). You will need to delete some of the rows from the page, which means this is probably a good place to explain how ClickFunnels pages are structured.

The structure of a ClickFunnels Page

A ClickFunnels page is made out of basic building blocks called Sections, Rows, Columns, and Elements. Each type of block has an associated color in the editor, and you can tell what you're looking at by the color of the border around it.

Now, the good thing is, ClickFunnels manages a lot of this for you automatically, and since you're using funnels that I have shared with you, you don't need to worry about it too much—it's just so you understand why things keep changing color as you click on different things in ClickFunnels!

For a much more in-depth understanding of this, along with dozens of sample funnels and layouts for the pages in them, get a FREE copy of Russell Brunson's *Funnel Hacker Cookbook*.

You can get it at http://brightflamebooks.com/FHCookbook

SECTIONS: Everything you see on a ClickFunnels page is held inside one or more Sections. Sections are the top level of a page, and they fill the whole width of the page in horizontal bands. You can have as many sections as you want, but there must always be at least one.

Sections are great for having the same background color or image for multiple rows. If you've ever seen a web page that seemed to have different horizontal zones as you scrolled down, that's achieved with sections.

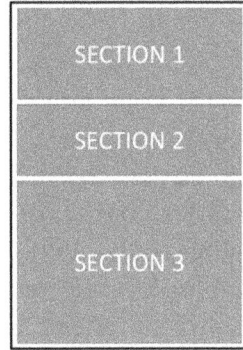

In the ClickFunnels editor, sections are associated with the color green—when you see a green border and icons, you know you're making changes to a section.

ROWS and COLUMNS: Every section must have at least one row in it to hold your "stuff". You can have a row with a single column that stretches across the whole section, or you can break it up into two or more columns. Any time you want to display your content in columns, you do it by creating a row with multiple columns.

In the ClickFunnels editor, rows and columns are associated with the color blue—when you see a blue border and icons, you know you're making changes to a row or column.

ELEMENTS: Elements are the actual things you see on the page: headlines, text, images, videos, buttons, Facebook comments panes, and everything else. These are housed in the rows and columns. You can add more than one element to a column. If you do, they are stacked vertically—that's why, if you want to show things next to each other, you have to create multiple columns in your row.

In the ClickFunnels editor, elements are associated with the color orange—when you see an orange border and icons, you know you're making changes to an element.

Deleting rows and sections

Let's say you want to delete the section labelled Step #4. If you hover your mouse over the header of that section, you'll see various borders and icon sets appear in different colors. If you let your mouse go near the edge of the section, where the white of the section turns to the grey background of the page, the border will turn green—this can sometimes be a bit fiddly in ClickFunnels, and you may need to move the mouse very carefully to get it.

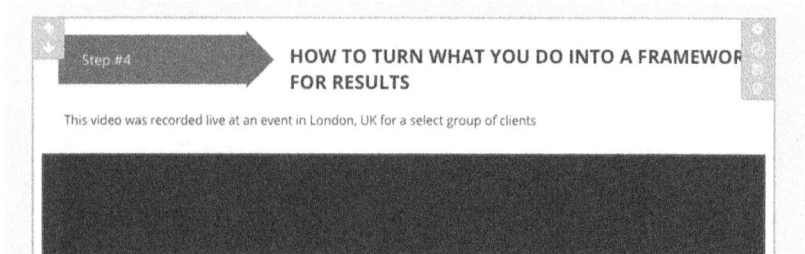

To delete the entire section, click the trashcan at the bottom of the group of four icons on the right. The section will disappear.

You can do the same with individual elements and whole rows. If you delete a column, the other columns in the row will expand to fill the space it leaves. Just hover over what you want to delete until the correct color border appears—blue for rows and columns, orange for elements—and click the trashcan.

Hiding a block

Now, sometimes you may not want to delete something; you may want to simply hide it so that you can bring it back later. For example, you may only have three bonuses now, but you know you'll be adding more later. It would make sense to hide the rows after the fourth, so you can restore them later as you add bonuses.

To do that, hover over whatever you want to hide, and when you see the appropriate color, click the Settings icon (the cog wheel).

For example, let's say you want to hide the row for the fourth bonus, which on the current page is the Story-Sell worksheet. As you hover your mouse over the row, you'll see the blue border appear — and you can see it's actually two columns.

To hide this, click on the ⚙ to open up the settings pane — when you're dealing with columns, the settings apply to all the columns in that row. At the bottom of the settings pane, notice the set of icons (which we've ignored up to now!).

- The ALL button, which is currently selected (you can tell because it's highlighted in blue), means that this row will be displayed on all devices — computers and mobile.

- If you want to make this row visible only on mobile de-vices—phones and tablets—select the second icon, which is a picture of a cellphone.
- Similarly, if you want this row to only be visible on computers—desktops and laptops—select the third icon, which shows a monitor. These two options are really useful if you have something on your page that doesn't look great on a mobile: you can create two versions, one for mobile and one for computers, and have ClickFun-nels pick which one to show based on how the visitor is browsing your page.
- The fourth icon—the eye—is the "Hide" icon. If you click this, the element will disappear in your editor and it won't be shown to anyone viewing the page.
- The hash/pound icon is for getting CSS info about the element—and if you don't know what that is, you'll never need to click this!
- The final icon—the trashcan—deletes this row.

So, to hide your row, click the eye icon and you're done.

But how do you bring it back, since it's disappeared?

Making the invisible visible

ClickFunnels maintains lists of all the parts of the page, visible and hidden. To bring back something that you've hidden, you need to find it in the appropriate list and unclick the eye icon. Look at the top menu on the page. You'll see buttons la-belled [SECTIONS], [ROWS], [COLUMNS], and [ELEMENTS].

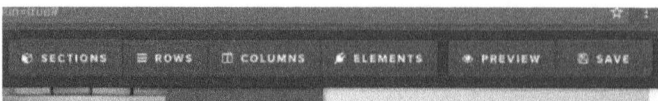

Since we have hidden a row and we want to bring it back, click on [ROWS], which brings up a submenu: <ADD ROW> and <MANAGE>. Click on <MANAGE> to bring up the list of every row on the page.

Look down the list until you find one with the eye icon greyed out—in the screenshot, it's the final one.

Click the eye so it's solid black again and your row will magically reappear.

Sections and Elements work in exactly the same way: click the button, click [MANAGE] and unhide whatever you want to restore.

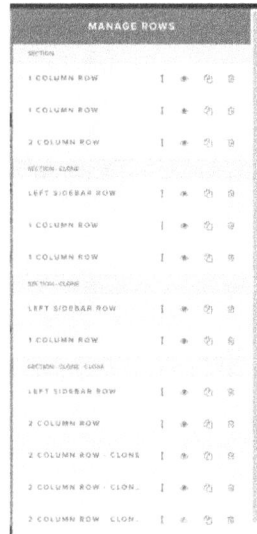

Adding upsells

Step #5 on the page lists all my other books. Each of the buttons links to the Amazon sales page for the book.

That's a really great way to drive sales of your other books. Remember: these are people who just bought one of your books, and you're giving them lots of free value, so they're great prospects to buy more from you. Another book is the easiest upsell.

Of course, you don't have to sell books. If you have products, you can link to the sales pages for those products, and if you don't have any products of your own, you can link to affiliate offers instead.

EXERCISE

Make the page your own

- Swap the cover image

- Swap the logo

- Swap the video

- Update the text

- Remove the graphical button if you don't need it, or redirect it to the Amazon review link for your book

- Edit the text button to point to your bonuses

- Edit Step 5 to point to your upsells

- Make any layout changes or content changes you need

19

Adding the Reader Bonus Autoresponder Sequence

When someone opts in, we want to send them a series of follow-up emails. We've already set up the Indoctrination sequence, which is to introduce them to you. However, we also want to send them emails specific to the bonuses they have just requested for your book.

As I said at the start of this book, I wanted to make process this as "Done For You" as I can, so I've created an ActiveCampaign automation that you can add directly into your account.

> If you're not using ActiveCampaign, you can download the text of the emails to copy and paste into your own email system. Visit this page to get them.
>
> **www.brightflamebooks.com/FunnelBonus**

Importing the email sequence in ActiveCampaign

To import the automation, log back into your ActiveCampaign account, go into <Automations>, and click on the [New Automation] button as though you were creating a new automation from scratch.

In the popup window, click on [Import Automation]

ActiveCampaign will ask you for the Automation URL. Enter the following: http://tplshare.com/U3LvmWU and click [IMPORT].

That opens an Automation Setup Wizard. Right now, the automation is defined based on what's in my ActiveCampaign system, so you need to adapt it to your own system. Click [GET STARTED], which will guide you through the necessary changes.

The wizard goes through each step in the sequence, asking appropriate questions for each one. For example, for each email it will ask what the sender name and email should be set to.

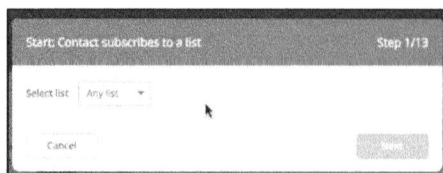

1. **"Start: Contact subscribes to list"** First, ActiveCampaign needs to know which list will trigger the automation. Click the dropdown menu next to Select List and pick your reader bonus list. Click [NEXT].
2. **"Send Email"** There are twelve emails in the sequence, so ActiveCampaign will ask you twelve times to enter the name and email address the email will be sent from. Assuming you only have one business email address, you can keep clicking [NEXT] on each screen and ActiveCampaign will fill this in automatically for you.

The twelve-day autoresponder is a mix of engagement, value-delivery, and pitching and upsell.

For each of the emails in the sequence, you'll have to go through and edit them to match your business. In each one, you'll find various bits of text marked out with {...}. As a minimum, you'll need to update those, but you'll probably want to change the wording and make each email "yours."

Also, some of the emails contain stories, and those will need to be replaced with your own stories, examples, and teaching points.

Here's an example: the first email, which is a relationship-building email.

Email #1 - Start building a Relationship

Email Subject: "{The Title}" - Your Gift Today

Hi %FIRSTNAME%,

Thank you for taking the time to enter your email, and thank you for reading my book.

Here are your bonuses for {book title}.

You signed up here and that is the reason you are getting this email: {Add your squeeze page link here}

Remember, as a buyer of {title}, I'm giving you the following valuable resources:

{list bonuses}

You can access them right now by clicking on this link: {Your bonus delivery link}

Go to this link ASAP and get your copy of {name of your first bonus} and the other resources.

And tomorrow be on the lookout for a special email called {name of your email tomorrow}

I want to make sure you see that email, because the information I'll share is so good, it's critical you open it up.

Thanks

{Your Name Here}

P.S. The download link to your bonuses will only be available for a short time. Download it today. {Your bonus delivery link}

The bonus delivery link

The final line of the email tells them how to get their bonuses, which in this case is the bonus delivery page in ClickFunnels. To get the correct link, go back into ClickFunnels. If you're still in the editor for the bonus delivery page, click [SAVE] and then the EXIT button in the top left. That will bring you back to the page overview.

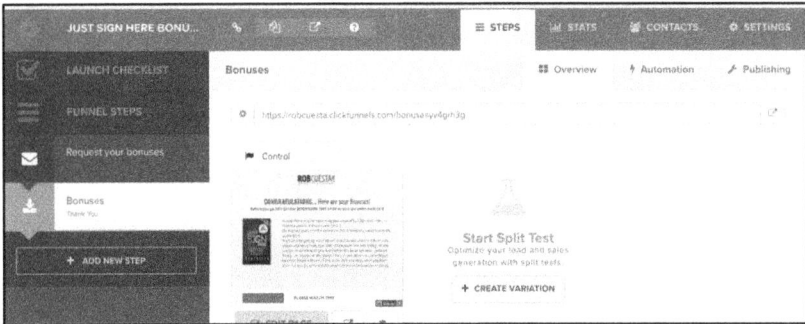

Just above the page thumbnail, you'll see a box with a URL. That is the specific URL for this page. Click in the box and select the URL, copy it, and paste it into your email in ActiveCampaign.

Make sure that you grab the URL for the Thank You page, not the Optin page: if you accidentally paste the wrong one into the email, your readers will be stuck in an infinite loop that keeps sending them back to opt in! **If you're not sure whether you've got the correct URL, paste it into a browser window and see where it takes you.**

The squeeze page link: You'll notice that I encourage you to include the link back to your optin page. Even though they've already signed up, it's a good idea to include this. They may not open your email immediately, and when they do, they may have forgotten that they asked for the information. If they have, then having the link there means they may click it, and when they see the page again it may jog their memory. To get the URL for this, the process is the same as for getting the Thank You page URL above, but select the Optin page in the left hand pane.

The First "Wait"

Earlier I showed you how to set up a simple wait for a specific length of time.

In this automation, there's a second wait with a condition. Combined, these two actions mean that ActiveCampaign will wait for one day, and if that falls on the subscriber's weekend, it will continue to wait until Monday.

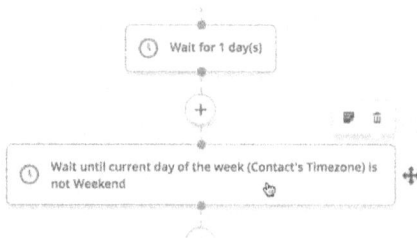

When you set up a Wait in ActiveCampaign, you have two options.

To set up a conditional wait, select the second option, which will bring up the Condition Editor where you can set conditions based on information about the contact or based on what is happening in the world. For example, you could keep someone in a Wait state until they are tagged with a specific value (e.g. to say that they have bought your new product).

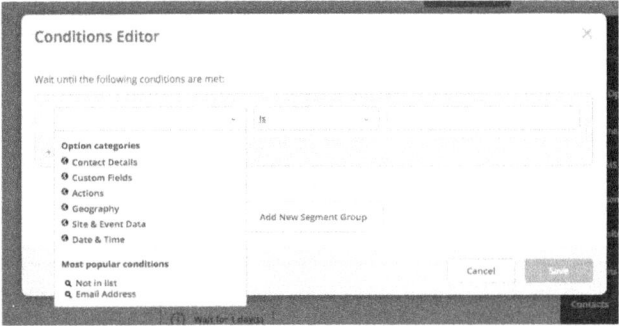

Click on any item in the dropdown list and it will open up the different data items you can use to set your condition. There are dozens of possibilities here, and it's beyond the scope of what you need for this funnel, but I just wanted you to be aware that the possibility is there.

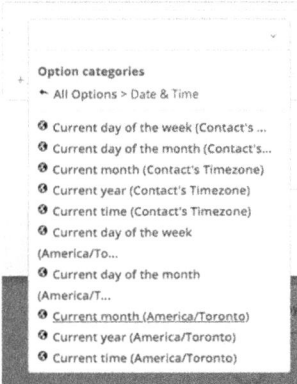

The one we have used here is the "Date & Time" option, specifically "Current day of the week (Contact's Time Zone)" to make sure our email only goes out on a weekday.

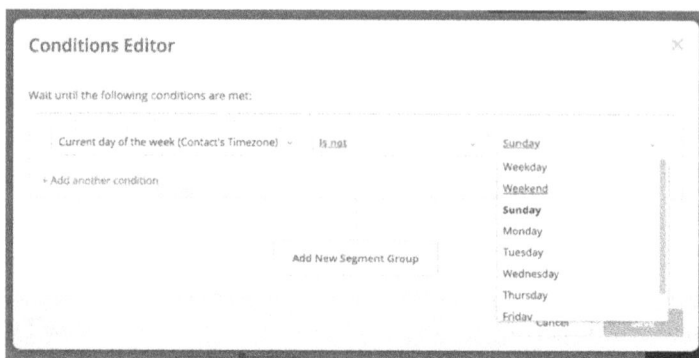

The rest of the sequence

Email 4 is a sales letter, which I have left deliberately blank. First, this is not a book about copywriting. Second, I don't know what you're selling. So, all I can tell you is where to put your pitch in the sequence, which is here and in Email 8.

NEED HELP WRITING POWERFUL COPY?

As I just said, this is not a book about writing copy. However, ClickFunnels offer a separate tool that will help you to create professional-level copy in minutes even if you've never written so much as a headline.

You can watch a demo of the software at

www.brightflamebooks.com/funnelscripts

The final email, #12, is a very interesting one because it basically says "Tell me what you want from me." Some people may well be on the verge of buying but they've just got one or two remaining questions. So, ask them what's on their mind. Their replies will give you their objections and also tell you what products they want you to create.

Email Subject: Can I ask for your help?

Hi %FIRSTNAME%

My main goal is to help you get the result you are looking for.

And I try and do that with all the valuable content I send you. You may have noticed all the tips and resources I deliver.

But I always want to help more, so I have a small favor to ask of you.

Over the next few weeks, I am going to put together the right information to help you succeed, and I want to deliver exactly what you want.

If you could, hit reply to this and let me know in a sentence or two the information that will help you succeed.

If enough people respond, I'll put that information in a free report to send out to you.

Thanks

{your name}

P.S. {insert deadline/urgency for buying your product} {your link here}

It's always worth asking that question to your list on a regular basis, and all I've done is fit that into this sequence.

Exercice

Import the 12-day automation into your email system and edit the emails to match your business.

Making the ClickFunnels URLs "Pretty"

The URLs ClickFunnels creates are, let's face it, ugly. You can set things up to use your own domain, but that requires some fairly technical setup.

If you have a WordPress website, you have two additional options.

1) Add a "Redirect" plugin. These allow you to create shortcuts that look like addresses on your website but actually go to a completely different page.
2) Add the ClickFunnels plugin. This is a redirect plugin built specifically for ClickFunnels pages.

Both are good options.

The ClickFunnels plugin "hides" the fact that the user is leaving your site, which is a good thing. However, there are certain pages that don't work through the plugin—specifically order forms—which is a bad thing. Also, you're restricted to ClickFunnels pages.

A redirect plugin—there are many in the WordPress repository—allows you to send the viewer anywhere on the web, but usually the address bar shows that they are no longer on the page.

To see both in action, try these links:

1) Redirect plugin:
   http://brightflamebooks.com/mastermind
2) ClickFunnels plugin:
   http://brightflamebooks.com/16ways

20

Set Your Funnel Free

If you've followed along this far, you have a reader bonus funnel ready to run.

Of course, a funnel is nothing without traffic. You can have the best funnel in the world, but unless someone goes to the page and enters their email address, it is useless.

Normally, I'd be saying something at this point along the lines of "Start running some Facebook ads" (or wherever your prospects are likely to be).

But a Reader Bonus funnel is different.

A reader bonus funnel isn't for cold traffic. It's for people who've read your book.

So, how do you get people to go from the book to the funnel?

You need a call to action.

At the start of this book, I showed you the call to action from my book *Premium!*

Here's the call to action at the end of my book *Authority!* It comes after several reminders throughout the book to register so you can download a resource that has just been mentioned.

Reader Bonuses

Remember!

Visit www.AuthorityExpertBook.com/register and confirm your purchase to get access to all the resources, guides and worksheets mentioned in this book.

You can also mark your calls to action out so that they are more noticeable. Just like this one!

Getting people to read your book

Once you've got your calls to action in place, you need to get those calls to action in front of readers. That's about how you sell copies of your book or how you use it in your direct marketing, both of which are beyond the scope of this book.

I have a program–the Author-Expert Insiders Circle–where I work with authors to help them monetize their book. You can find out more about it at

www.HowExpertsGetClients.com

How many calls to action, and where?

One of the biggest questions I get from clients is "How many calls to action should I have?" closely followed by "Where should my calls to action go?" (Sadly, I've even had people ask, "Do I really need a call to action?")

I've seen all sorts of advice given by different gurus online, ranging from "put one in every chapter" to "just put one at the end."

Ultimately, the answer is "it depends": it depends on your audience, on the length of the book, and on the call to action.

If you're using your book to grow your business, you absolutely need calls to action (CTAs) throughout your book. That's a hard steer that I give all our ghostwriting and publishing clients.

The reason is simple: It lets you know that someone who read your book is interested in something more.

When you give your book to a potential client, if they act on one of the CTAs, you know that something in your book hit home, and your offer was interesting. That information is gold dust: they are telling you that they're a warm — potentially even a hot — lead.

Those are the people you need to be prioritizing for follow up.

Better yet, rather than saying to someone, "Here's my book. I'll call you in a couple of weeks to see what you thought," you can give them the book and say, "Here's my book. There are some additional resources that make it even more useful, and if you want them there's instructions in the book for getting them."

What's the difference?

In the first scenario, you're the one chasing. In the second, they're coming to you. Which do you think gives you the better chance of closing a sale?

Finding out who bought your book

When someone buys your book on Amazon, CTAs are even more important. If someone searched Amazon (or Barnes & Noble, or iBooks, or wherever), chose your book, and—most important of all—paid for it, they are a **red-hot lead** for you. The problem is, retailers don't tell you who those people are, so you can't follow up.

You have to have a mechanism in place for finding out who bought your book, and that's the CTAs.

That's why I'm always surprised when a client pushes back on the idea of putting CTAs in their book. I've heard every excuse under the sun, but the three most common are:

1. "My readers will be put off by calls to action."
2. "My audience doesn't respond to calls to action."
3. "I don't want to come across as salesy."

These are all nonsense. Readers are only put off by calls to action that are irrelevant, unappealing (like "subscribe to my newsletter"), and don't offer real value. I don't care whether your audience is CEOs of Fortune 100 companies, expectant mothers, college students, or any other demographic: they won't respond to worthless, dull, irrelevant calls to action, but they *will* respond if you offer them something that appeals to them, that is relevant, and has real value.

> If your audience doesn't respond to your calls to action, it's *your* fault, not theirs.

And in the same way, if your CTAs are inherently self-serving ("Want to hire us? Call xxx") then you'll come across as salesy. You can put one or two direct actions like that in your book, but beyond that, you'll put people off.

The answer to all three excuses is the same: you need to make interesting, appealing, valuable, relevant offers. When you do that, readers will be *grateful* for it, even if you have one in every single chapter.

But you have to be smart with your calls to action.

Let's say your call to action is "register your book to get all these bonuses..." followed by a bullet list of your entire bonus stack. If you put that after every chapter, readers will start to block it out after about the fourth chapter. So, I usually tell my clients to put the full "get all these bonuses" call to action in their book twice: at the start and end. If it's a long book—over 150 pages or so—you may get away with a third one roughly halfway through the book.

If your book is very short—less than 60 pages, say—that may be all you need. But for a book longer than 60 pages, you are going to need a few more calls to action. How do you do that without repeating the full bonus stack offer?

The single most valuable technique I've discovered for doing that is what I call "Chapter Upgrades."

Chapter Upgrades as Calls to Action

The idea of chapter upgrades is simple. In exchange for their contact details, you offer your reader a piece of bonus content that will *enhance* and *supplement* what they've just read. Unlike newsletters and free reports, it's specifically designed to help them apply the information in the chapter.

When you do that, you can put a CTA into every chapter if you want, and people won't mind.

Great chapter upgrades include resource lists, quizzes and assessments, infographics, recipes/how to's, videos, and expert interviews. But almost anything can be used as an offer: the main requirement is that it must be specific to the chapter.

Another really interesting chapter upgrade is a video summary of the chapter, which I mentioned earlier in the book. This appeals to people's innate desire for instant consumption. If, at the start of each chapter, you offer readers the option of simply watching a short video that summarizes what they're about to read, most people will jump at it.

Because they are seen as high-value and relevant, the conversion rate for chapter upgrades is very high. In a world where newsletters and free reports typically get 1-2% optin, chapter upgrades can get anything from 20-50% optin.

And because of the variety of resources offered, even if a reader isn't interested in the offer for one chapter, there's a good chance one or more of the other offers will grab their attention.

When you do this — when you create chapter-specific resources as bonuses — you're building your bonus stack without having to think about it. By the time you've written ten chapters and created a bonus for each, you have ten bonuses you can list at the start and end of your book. And you can mention them as you go without annoying your readers or coming across as salesy.

And by the way, you don't have to create separate funnels for each chapter: send them to a single optin page and put all the bonuses on the delivery page.

Exercise

Write the calls to action for you book.

Add the bonuses to your Reader Bonus Funnel delivery page in Click-Funnels

21

Conclusion

We made it!

It's been quite a journey—and the book is, surprisingly, already much longer than I thought it would be(!) but think about what you've achieved so far.

You have learned

- how to set up a list in ActiveCampaign
- how to send broadcast emails
- how to create automated multi-step follow-up sequences
- how to create templates and signatures for your emails
- how to link ActiveCampaign to ClickFunnels
- how to work with pictures and buttons in ClickFunnels
- how to work with headlines and text boxes
- how to add a video to your ClickFunnels page
- how to add a downloadable file to ClickFunnels

And much more!

All of these are skills you will reuse in the next part of our book, where we set up your Free + Shipping funnel.

PART FOUR

Setting Up Your Free + Shipping Funnel

22

The Free + Shipping Funnel

The big idea behind the Free + Shipping Funnel is that a lead is much more valuable if they've paid you something — even if all they've paid is $7.95. As I said earlier, a buyer is a buyer is a buyer. The very hardest sale with any customer is the first. Once someone has bought something, it's much easier to get them to buy again. But it's that first purchase that's critical.

In a free + shipping funnel, you offer your visitor a free copy of your book and you ask them to cover the cost of shipping it to them. It's a reasonable request, but it instantly turns people who were looking for free information into buyers. Better yet, not only has the visitor now paid you something, but you can make the offer pay for itself. Let's say your book costs $4 to print and $3 to ship. You can charge $7.95 for shipping and handling and use the small profit you make on most buyers to pay for the extra shipping cost to overseas buyers.

Where it fits

The free + shipping funnel takes someone all the way from being a Visitor to being a Buyer. And the reason you want and need a Free + Shipping funnel is simple: because you'll sell more stuff and make more money.

Where it fits
(The Client Journey)

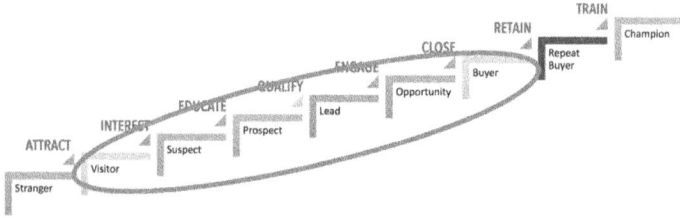

Russell Brunson—the creator of ClickFunnels—ran a test where he drove 100 visitors to a sales page for a $197 product. What he found was that 1% of visitors bought from the page, so for every 100 visitors, he made $197. When he put in a free + shipping offer, however, 8% of visitors took the offer, and 25% of those buyers then *also bought the product*—in other words, 2% of visitors paid the $197, so for every 100 visitors, he made $394. It ended up doubling the sales of the product.

Why you want one

THE 100 VISITOR TEST

Because you'll sell more stuff and make more money!

Now, your funnel, your book, and your industry are different, so I can't tell you that you'll double your sales, but I can tell you that a free + shipping offer will generally raise the sales. And it happens because it's really easy to get people to ask for a

<u>free</u> book and pay for the shipping. And once they've paid you, it becomes much easier to get them to then buy the upsell.

Free plus shipping offers are also extremely useful if you're in a situation where you can't put a call to action into your book. For example, if you published through a traditional publisher and your book has been out for a while, it's difficult—if not impossible—to get them to change the book, especially if the only change you want to make is a call to action that's going to benefit you but not the publisher.

So, rather than waiting for people to read the book and tell you they're interested by registering, advertise that people can get your book for free and get them to tell you upfront that they're interested. In other words, if you can't find out who bought your book after they bought it, use a free + shipping funnel to find out who bought your book *as* they buy it.

If you're with a traditional publisher, you probably don't get to buy your books at cost; instead, you have an author discount, which means you may have to make a small loss on the cost of sending the book out. In a little while, however, I'll show you how to make that money back later in the funnel. Deal?

The Big Picture

Here's what's happening in the free + shipping funnel.

1. Someone comes to your offer page.
2. They enter their credit card, shipping details, and you can even add a low-cost order bump (you probably saw one of those when you first signed up for ClickFunnels).

3. You put them through a series of onetime offers.
4. They end up at a Thank You page with what's called an "offer wall" (like the panel with all my books at the end of the Reader Bonus delivery page).

The Big Picture

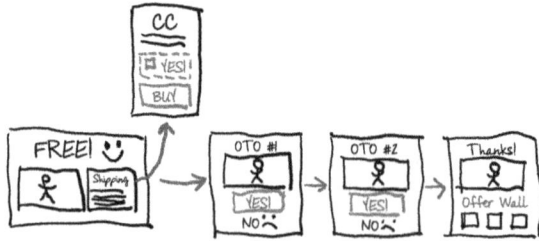

Just as I did with the Reader Bonus funnel, I've shared a pre-configured funnel with you to make things easy for you. I've deliberately kept that funnel simple, so there's only one upsell page. That way, you only have to think of one product to offer.

To grab the shared Free + Shipping Funnel, simply visit

http://brightflamebooks.com/freebookshare

(This time, you don't need to use an incognito window).

What you need

In order to set up this funnel, you'll need the following:

- A book to ~~sell~~ give away
- A cover image or 3D image
- An upsell

- Sales videos for the book and upsells
- More stuff to sell (for the offer wall)
- A follow-up sequence (which I'll give you)
- A payment processing account
- Screenshots of your best Amazon reviews
- Traffic

Traffic

When we discussed the Reader Bonus funnel, I said that all the traffic comes from your book, so you need to work on distribution of your book. With the Free + Shipping funnel, you can use two kinds of traffic

1) Cold traffic—you can run ads to send people to the funnel, and also put the link on your website
2) Warm traffic—you can send the link to subscribers already on your list.
3) Partners—ask other people to tell their list about your free book offer.

This is a great way, as I said above, of getting people to make their first purchase. That applies equally to people who have been on your list for a while but haven't bought: you can send them an email telling them about your offer and some of them will finally cross the line to become buyers. Even better, if you know that you're paying $1 per click, you can just add that dollar onto the shipping charge and now you have a funnel that not only pays for what you're sending out, it also pays for the advertising to get people there. So, it becomes what's known as a self-liquidating offer.

Russell Brunson's Expert Secrets

Here's the page for Russell Brunson's *Expert Secrets* which demonstrates everything I'm going to be talking about.

See the original page at

www.brightflamebooks.com/expertsecrets

Ryan Levesque's Ask

Here's another example, the free + shipping page for Ryan Levesque's book *Ask*, which is an excellent book about using quizzes and surveys in your marketing. (something EVERY author should be doing!)

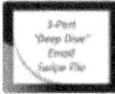

Claim Your FREE Book Now and Get These FREE Training Bonuses

BONUS ONE

BONUS TWO

BONUS THREE

BONUS FOUR

BONUS FIVE

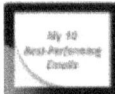

The button marked "YES! I want my free copy of Ask!" opens the order page. However, some people may want more information before committing, so he lists all the bonuses.

There's also a section near the top of the page ("When Will I Receive My Book?") that explains how long people will have to wait for their book. That will avoid quite a few support emails from people who think you're waiting at the corner of their street for them to order so you can run down and drop it in their mailbox before they've even shut down their browser window—although you'll still get them, even if you put something like that on your page.

Down the side of the page are lots of reviews, which provide social proof and will help tip a few more people "over the edge" to buy.

The $1 Book Funnel

There's another variant on Free + Shipping, and that's the $1 Book Funnel, which has been used extensively by GKIC (now No-BS Inner Circle), one of the most successful business coaching organizations in the world.

As the name suggests, the idea here is that you ask people to pay just $1, which makes it even easier to get someone to make that first purchase, but it does carry some risk for you.

Obviously, there's no way $1 is going to even cover your shipping cost, let alone the cost of printing the books, so you're making a loss on every single book you send. It's simply about getting them to pay something—anything—and become a buyer. To make this work, you really need to know your numbers. Specifically, you need to know the value of a lead.

When somebody orders the book from GKIC, they are offered what the company calls The Most Incredible Free Gift Ever, which is a free two-month subscription to their continuity program and a bundle of products.

Now, they've done this for so long that they know exactly what percentage of people who buy the book will keep subscribing, and for how long. So, they know how much they will make, and they know that they can afford to make that $1 offer for the book.

If you want to run this kind of funnel, set it up initially as a Free + Shipping offer while you figure out how many people take the upsells. Then, once you've tweaked the offer and you know your funnel is profitable, you can drop the price to $1.

Taking Payments

Before we go any further, make sure you have a way to take payments from your visitors using ClickFunnels.

My personal recommendation—and I urge all my clients to use it—is Stripe (stripe.com). It's a well-established, stable platform that integrates with many other systems, including Click-Funnels.

Setting up an account with Stripe is free. They take a fee from each payment they process, and it's in line with most other online payment processors.

Most importantly, however, they are very easy to deal with. If you've ever had problems with other companies—especially a very well-known one whose name suggests they're your pay "friend"—you'll appreciate the fact that there's no monthly or annual fees, they pay you your money automatically, and they won't shut you down if you suddenly become successful and start making more money.

Integrating Stripe with ClickFunnels

If you're following my advice, ClickFunnels has detailed instructions on how to integrate your Stripe account at http://bit.ly/2MV9RUS.

If you prefer to use a different payment processor, check whether it's supported and how to integrate it at http://bit.ly/2tUh0xx.

Adding reviews

Before we start working on the funnel, there's one critical piece of prep work to do.

Because we are going to be sending cold traffic to the page, it's important to add some social proof to the page. If you have them, Amazon reviews of your book are very powerful, because they're perceived to be independent.

If your book isn't on Amazon, or it's very new and you don't have any reviews yet, you can use testimonials as an alternative, but they may not be as convincing because they're about you, not the book. A better alternative is to get some endorsements of the book from people you know — especially if they're from influencers that your audience recognizes — but in the end you are going to need to get some Amazon reviews for your book, if only because your book will not sell on Amazon without them.

Assuming you do have some reviews, however, pick the best ones and take some screenshots of them.

★★★★★ **The single best book I have read on developing a coaching business**
By JP Jakonen on February 19, 2015
Format: Kindle Edition   Verified Purchase

This is, not by far, but is anyway, THE SINGLE BEST BOOK on business positioning, business models and marketing I have read. My Kindle version has 40 notes, mostly "Ooooohhh!"s and "Aaaaaaah!"s, since that's what reading this book did to me: constant revelations of how I really could transform my business.

I can't understand why there are only a few reviews of this book! Having read + being influenced by small business and marketing gurus like Dan Kennedy, Alan Weiss, C.J. Hayden, Jonn Jantsch, Michael Gerber, Robert Cialdini and Claude Hopkins, I still rank this as the best book I've read on how to develop my coaching business to a new level.

But, enough!

I will post a new follow-up review exactly one month from now and let you know what and how I've implemented Rob's thoughts. And, what has it done to actually grow my business.

FOLLOW-UP: One month after reading Premium! (29.3.2015)

What's great about Rob's thinking in Premium! is that it matches my own. But - and here's the important part - it's my emergent thinking, something that I see as a future model, a new way of being. Truly priceless.
Since reading Premium! I invested in Rob's VIP DAY course. Having gone through 1/2 of the program, I have already booked a client company for my own VIP Day.

This guy is really a gem. Listen to what he says. It will make your coaching/expert business just so much better. I am so glad I found this book!

▸ Comment   One person found this helpful. Was this review helpful to you?   [Yes]   [No]   Report abuse

★★★★★ **Awesome Bonuses Included!**
By SigriddK on December 2, 2014
Format: Kindle Edition   Verified Purchase

That's a great book and obviously written by someone who knows what they are talking about! ..but wait, there's more! The in-Book Bonuses are mind blowing. Read it and you'll be well on your way to higher income!

▸ Comment   Was this review helpful to you?   [Yes]   [No]   Report abuse

★★★★★ **Awesome book!**
By Mark A Hicks on October 1, 2014
Format: Kindle Edition   Verified Purchase

You'll learn a lot from this book. Well worth it.

▸ Comment   One person found this helpful. Was this review helpful to you?   [Yes]   [No]   Report abuse

★★★★★ **Lots of breakthrough ideas for experts.**
By Robert Rolih on September 28, 2014
Format: Kindle Edition   Verified Purchase

Great book for experts who want to make more money. In the first half of the book I already got two breakthrough ideas for my seminar business. This book can really challenge you to think differently about your business.

Adding the Funnel to Your System

If you haven't done it already, grab the Free + Shipping Funnel that I've shared with you.

> ## Simply visit
> http://brightflamebooks.com/freebookshare

This time, you don't need to use an incognito window — simply open the link in your browser. If you're logged into ClickFunnels, the funnel will be added to your system automatically. If you're not, it will ask you to log in.

If it looks like it's asking you to create a new account, look for a link that says anything along the lines of "Already a member? Log in"

And if after all of that you're still struggling, log into Click-Funnels first and try again.

23

Page 1 – The Order Page

The sample Page I've shared with you contains the main elements you'll need: the shipping and payment box, a video, bullet points, and an area for your reviews.

What we're going to do

Here are the modifications you'll make to the order page:

- Add your own video
- Add your cover image
- Change the copy
- Add your Amazon reviews screenshot
- Change the background of the offer section
- Change the copyright notice
- Connect the page to the Free + Shipping list in Active-Campaign

Most of these you already know how to do, and the skills that are new are really variations on things that you already know. See? I told you at the end of the Reader Bonus Funnel that you'd already learned most of what you needed!

Editing the page

The first step to modifying your order page is to open it up for editing, exactly as we saw in *Opening a funnel* on page 124. So, go to the list of Funnels in ClickFunnels, and click on the new funnel (which will be called "Sample Free + Shipping") to open it for editing.

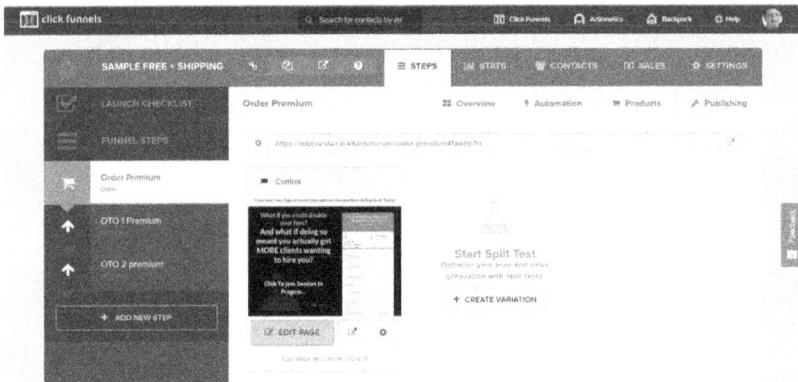

Changing the page name

At the moment, the page is called "Order Premium" — which I'm guessing you will want to change!

Near the top left corner, you'll see a menu item <Publishing>. Click that to open the options for this page.

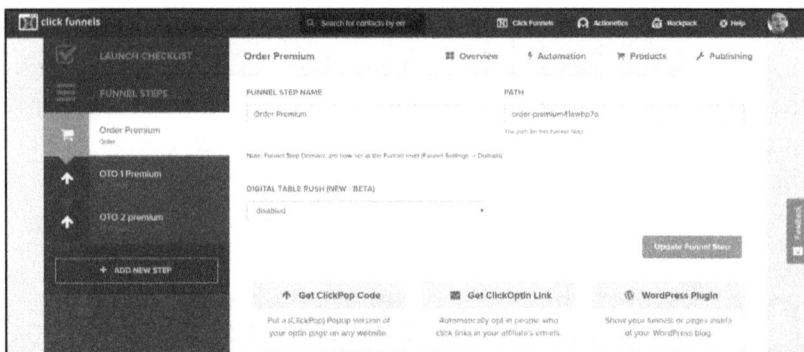

Near the top, you'll see a box labelled "FUNNEL STEP NAME": type the new name into there (You are the only person who sees this, so you can make it as meaningful as you want).

Notice that changing the step name won't update the path to the page — that's an unfortunate feature of ClickFunnels, but most visitors will never notice, especially if you use a redirect plugin to hide the system URLs, as I suggested in *Making the ClickFunnels URLs "Pretty"* on page 170.

Editing page content

To get back to editing our page, simply click <Overview> to take you back to the main screen for this page, and click on the [EDIT PAGE] button below the thumbnail.

Most of the text on the page is edited as it was for the Reader Bonus Funnel.

1. The "Claim your free copy" banner at the top of the page. This is a simple text box, so you can click on the text and replace it with your own words.
2. The headlines above the video. These are standard headlines, so you can overtype them as well.
3. The "Get Your Free Copy" box at the top of the shipping form. This, too, is a standard headline. Below, I'll explain how to change the contents of the shipping form.
4. The video: You can swap this for your own, just as you did on the Reader Bonus delivery page.
5. "You cover the shipping...", "Tell me where to ship...", "Premium will help you to...". These are all headlines. Below, I'll tell you how to change the bullet points and the background image.
6. The "HURRY!..." bar. This is a simple headline.
7. "The single best read..." This is another headline. The text is an excerpt from one of the reviews. Replace it with a compelling snippet of your own review or endorsement.
8. "YES! Send me my free copy!" This is a button. Edit it the same way you edited buttons on the Reader Bonus funnel delivery page.
9. The "Get Your Free Book" arrow: This is an image. You can show this to a designer on Fiverr and get them to create a version with your own book cover on it.
10. The reviews: This is an image. Replace it with the screenshot of your own reviews that I got you to take earlier on.
11. The copyright notice: Overtype the text with your own business name and replace the hyperlink with a link to your own page. Depending on the laws in your country

of residence, you may also need to add links to your terms of service and privacy policy.

> The video on this page is very specific to Premium. However, it will serve as a guide to the kind of things you need to cover. To download a copy of the script, Visit:
>
> **www.brightflamebooks.com/FunnelBonus**

Here's what's new:

- The order form
- The bullet points
- The background headshot halfway down the page

The Order Form

ClickFunnels provides us with a pre-built two-step order form widget specifically for these types of pages. The idea behind these forms is simple. They're designed to activate Cialdini's commitment and consistency principle (which I discussed above) to increase conversion. So, in the first step you get the visitor to enter their contact details first, which feels like a low-commitment action, and it's only once they proceed to step 2 that you ask for their payment details.

When you open the options pane for the form (by clicking on it), the fields are pretty self-explanatory. Most of the fields relate to the shipping address and contact details. The rest relate to the button on each step.

At the top, **PREVIEW STEPS** allows you to switch between the two panels in the editor preview.

If you select [Step #1], you'll see the shipping form. You can change labels on this step, but you can't change the overall design—for example, you can't add or remove fields.

This options pane has a lot of fields, so to make it easier, there are two drop downs that allow you to show or hide sets of options. **EDIT STEP #1**, just below PREVIEW STEPS, lets you hide or show the fields specific to Step #1 of the order form.

If you want to change the button text or the color of the button, scroll down on the options pane. The labels on the button for step 1 are controlled by the fields STEP #1 BTN TEXT and STEP #1 BTN SUB TEXT. The text below the button is controlled by BUTTON FOOTER TEXT.

When you finish editing step 1, go back to the top and use the EDIT STEP #1 dropdown to hide the options for this step.

If you can't see options for step 2, use **EDIT STEP #2** to show the next set of options. At the same time, switch PREVIEW STEPS to Step #2 and you'll see the form change in the editor.

			SUMMARY ITEM TEXT	Item
PREVIEW STEPS	Step #1	Step #2		
			SUMMARY PRICE TEXT	
EDIT STEP #1	Hide Step #1 Setting	⌄		amount
EDIT STEP #2	Show Step #2 Settin	⌄		
			BUMP HEADLINE	Yes, I will Take It!
STEP #2 HEADLINE	your info		OTO HEADLINE	ONE TIME OFFER
STEP #2 SUB HEADLINE			OTO TEXT	Lorem ipsum dolor sit amet,
	Your Billing Info		STEP #2 BTN TEXT	Complete Order
SELECT ITEM TEXT	Item		STEP #2 BTN SUB TEXT	
SELECT PRICE TEXT	Price			Step #2 BTN Sub Text
CC NUMBER TEXT	Credit Card Number:		BUTTON FOOTER TEXT	
CC CVC TEXT	CVC:			* 100% Secure & Safe Payme
			BACK TO SHIPPING TEXT	
CC EXP. MONTH TEXT	Expiry Month:			Edit Shipping Details
CC EXP. YEAR TEXT	Expiry Year:		FONT FAMILY	OPEN SANS
FORM CC TEXT	Card number		BUTTON TEXT	
FORM CVC TEXT	CVC		BUTTON COLOR	

The top set of fields are all related to credit card details, so you probably won't need to change these.

Scrolling down, however, you'll find some more interesting options.

SUMMARY ITEM TEXT and **SUMMARY ITEM PRICE** control what is shown in the table below the credit card details.

I'll come back to the next three options— **BUMP HEADLINE, OTO HEADLINE** and **OTO TEXT**—in a moment.

STEP #2 BTN TEXT and SUB TEXT work the same as for Step 1, as does BUTTON FOOTER TEXT.

BACK TO SHIPPING TEXT is displayed at the top of the form and allows the user to go back and edit the information they gave in Step 1.

FONT FAMILY, BUTTON TEXT color and BUTTON COLOR apply to both Step 1 and Step 2—the system enforces consistency across the screens, which is always a good thing (it helps conversion).

Adding a One-Time-Offer/Upsell

The three options I skipped above—BUMP HEADLINE, OTO HEADLINE and OTO TEXT—allow you to add an instant upsell to this page, which is a great way of increasing the value of your leads instantly. For example, you could offer the audio version of your book, a workbook, a video course, or some other product that readers of your book are likely to want.

To create an OTO, first go to the [ADVANCED] tab of the settings pane. That will open up a new set of options.

The lower options allow you to change the look and feel of

the form: feel free to play with these and see what happens.

The top three options give you control over some of the content of the form.

If you don't want to collect phone numbers from your buyers, **TOGGLE PHONE #** allows you to turn that field off.

If you have a digital product that doesn't require shipping, you can similarly use **TOGGLE SHIPPING** to turn off the address fields, so that step one only collects the buyer's name, email and (possibly) phone number.

TOGGLE ORDER BUMP allows you to add an on-page upsell.

If you change the dropdown to "Show Order Bump", a new section appears on Step 2 of the order form.

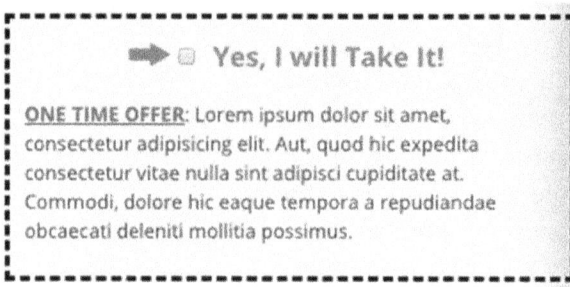

To change the details the offer, go back to the main [SETTINGS] tab at the top of the settings pane.

BUMP HEADLINE changes the green text next to the checkbox.

OTO HEADLINE changes the underlined red text.

OTO Text changes the main paragraph.

The key to a good order bump is that it should be an impulse purchase. So, it has to be something the buyer is definitely going to want if they want the book, and it has to have a low price—typically $7 to $37. If you want to sell something for more than that, you'll probably want to put that in a later page and do some more selling, in which case the order bump is an excellent way to bridge the gap from a small shipping charge to a $200+ offer.

If you decide you don't want an order bump, you can turn the toggle off again in the [ADVANCED] tab.

Setting up the shipping charge (and any OTO)

Shipping and OTOs are treated as products. To set the shipping fee, come out of the editor and come back to the overview screen for the page.

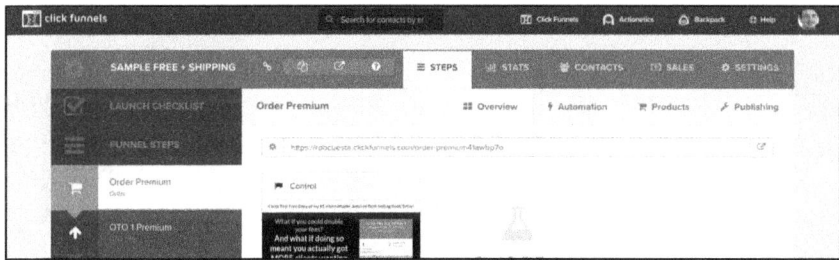

Click on the [Products] tab and then click the [+ Add Product] button.

By the way, these two-step order forms are not specifically created for free + shipping offers: you can use them to sell anything. That's why you have to set up the shipping charge as a product: it's just something being sold on this order form.

ADD NEW PRODUCT   X

O° Settings   Fulfillment Email   Email Integration   Shipping

Name

[   ]

Billing Integration   To change which stripe account is used, visit the settings for this funnel. ⓘ

[Stripe Account-My Stripe Account   ]

Amount

[0.00]

Amount Currency   now supporting 138 currencies (beta) ⓘ

[USD   ]

Price Display On Order Form   (optional) override the display of the price on order form. ⓘ

[$25 / 3 Months]

Should This Product Be The Bump On The Order Page?

[ ] Should this product be the bump on the order page if present?

Stripe Integration
○ Subscription ◉ One Time

Product Description   limited to 22 characters. ⓘ

[   ]

This will appear on your customers credit card statement alongside your company name that you set in your Payment Gateway settings.

                                                        CREATE PRODUCT

In the **name** field, enter "Shipping and handling". If you want to charge different rates for domestic and overseas buyers, you can simply create separate products and give them appropriate names (e.g. "Shipping - US" and "Shipping – Rest of World").

Enter the **amount** you want to charge and set the **currency**.

The **Price Display** field allows you to control how the price is shown on screen. For a single payment like this, you can leave it blank.

As this is the shipping charge, leave Should This Product Be The Bump On The Order Page? unchecked.

The next set of fields will depend on the payment processor you've chosen. The screenshot above shows what you see when you have Stripe set up (as I recommended earlier). If you're using Stripe, select **One Time** and then add a **Product Description**. This is what will be shown in the buyer's credit card statement, so try to make it meaningful and recognizable, otherwise you may end up with chargebacks, which is never a good thing! Once you've filled in all the fields, click [Fulfillment Email] to go to the next step.

Fulfilment Email

Any time someone buys a product through ClickFunnels, they get a fulfillment email from the system.

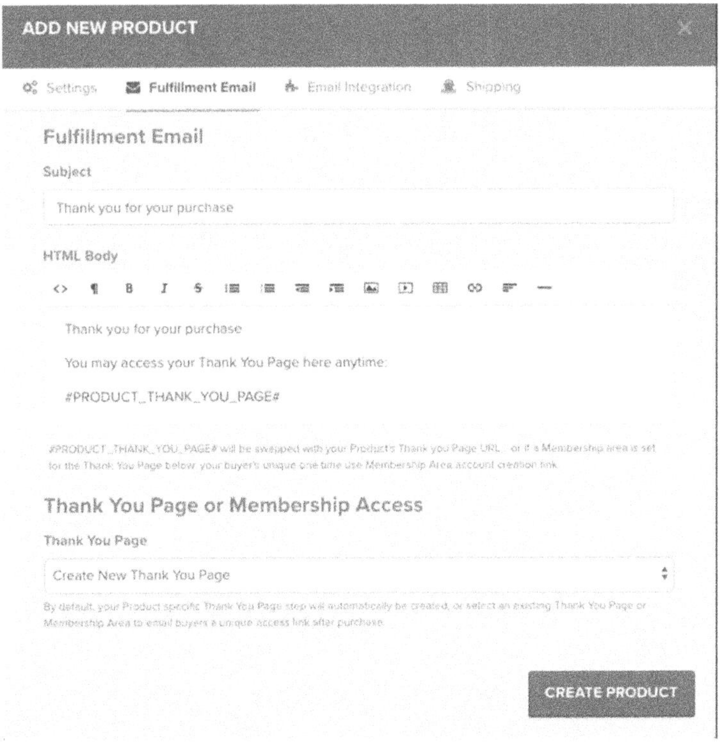

If you were selling a digital product, of course, you would send them the URL of the login page. As this is simply a book, however, you can delete all the content in the HTML Body box and write a simple note that lets them know what happens next. Remember: this email is simply for the shipping. It doesn't include the order bump, which they may or may not have picked (we'll talk about the email for that in a moment). For example, when people get my Premium book, they get a simple email that says

SUBJECT: Thank you for your purchase

Thank you for your purchase. You'll get a confirmation of your order shortly.

All the best

Rob Cuesta

For shipping, you can ignore the **THANK YOU PAGE or MEMBERSHIP ACCESS** field and simply click on [Email Integration] in the menu to continue.

Email Integration

This is the screen where you're going to add buyers to a list. All you're going to do is pick ActiveCampaign (or whichever email system you use), In the next box, ACTION ON SUBMIT, select "Add to list".

And in the LIST TO ADD LEAD box, pick the Free + Shipping list that you set up earlier. If the list isn't shown, click just below that, where it says "REFRESH LIST FROM API" to force

ActiveCampaign to fetch information from ActiveCampaign (and if you didn't set it up before, go back to *Creating your first list* on page 45 and set it up now).

Shipping

The shipping options are integrations with two companies that deliver CDs and DVDs (Kunaki and DiscDelivered.com). So, despite the name, they're not relevant for this funnel!

Changing the bullet points

Bullet points are a separate content type in ClickFunnels. That was a smart choice by the coding team, since it means we can use all sorts of special characters as bullets, make them a different font size from the text, and even have them in a contrasting color.

Editing the text of the bullet points themselves is simple — it works just like a ClickFunnels text box. To edit the bullets, however, click in the bullet list, then click the cog wheel in the top right. That will open the bullet options pane.

The **SETTINGS** pane lets you pick the font, font size, and color for your bullet points, and the color of the bullets. You can also define a separate color to be used for text that is bold, which is great for making it really stand out. And you can add some vertical space at the top using the **TOP MARGIN** slider.

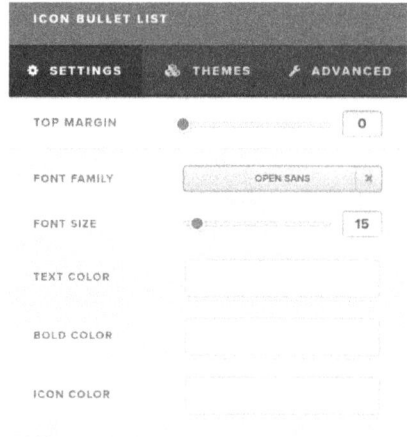

To choose the character that is used for the bullets, you have to go to the **ADVANCED** pane, however.

At first, this screen is confusing, because you can see multiple identical **ICON PICKER** fields.

If you count the number of fields, however, you'll realize that you have one for each bullet point in your list. So, if you wanted to have different bullets for each line — say check marks for some and crosses for others — you can.

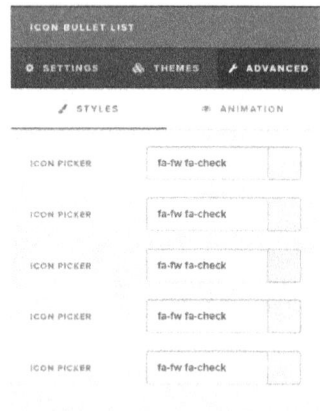

To pick the specific icon that will be used for a point, click any of the grey boxes on the right-hand end of the corresponding ICON PICKER field.

Of course, you'll need to write your own copy for the bullets to "sell" you book!

NEED HELP WITH WRITING COPY?

ClickFunnels offers a separate tool that will help you create pro-level copy even if you've never written so much as a headline. It even includes wizards for creating compelling bullet points!

If you don't know copywriting it's a great way to save yourself a LOT of time. You can watch a demo at
www.brightflamebooks.com/funnelscripts

24

Sending the book

One of the key reasons why I recommend ActiveCampaign over free/cheap alternatives is the ability to send a notification email to someone other than the email subscriber.

I mentioned this briefly earlier in the book.

Under Sending Options in Active Campaign (page 75), one of the options is to send a notification. Normally in an automation, we are emailing the subscriber — indeed, in most email systems that's ALL you can do. A Notification, however, is an email that is sent to someone else when the subscriber reaches that point in the automation. That could be you, a team member, an assistant, or even a third-party supplier

The beauty of those notifications is that it allows us to integrate offline and online follow-up activities. For example, you can set up a notification email that tells you to send the prospect a postcard, then a few days later, another email to tell you to send a printed sales letter, and a few days after that a third email that tells your fulfilment company to send them a DVD. And in between, of course, you can be sending emails and SMS messages to the subscriber.

In this case, you are going to send yourself a single email immediately after someone pays for shipping to tell you to send them the book. The email I created for you in the automation simply says that someone has paid and gives you their email. You'll then need to log into ClickFunnels and get their shipping address — I'll show you how in a moment.

If you use Zapier.com, you can zap the buyer's address details into your ActiveCampaign database, in which case you can insert those details into the email. That's a more elegant solution. But, since I can't assume everyone reading this book has Zapier, I have kept things as simple as possible.

A note about Zapier

If you've ever felt frustrated trying to keep different systems in sync, you'll love Zapier. I call it "plumbing for the internet." Zapier is a system that integrates with many different online platforms and allows you to do something in one system when a trigger action happens in another system—a lot like the integrations we are using send contact details from ClickFunnels to ActiveCampaign, but with a lot more control.

Their free account will allow you to set up the transfer for shipping details, so if you want to try it out, head over to www.zapier.com and get started.

Getting shipping details from ClickFunnels

When someone buys a product in ClickFunnels — and remember our shipping charges are set up as a product — their details are stored in the ClickFunnels database.

To access those details, click on [ClickFunnels] in the top menu, then select [Sales].

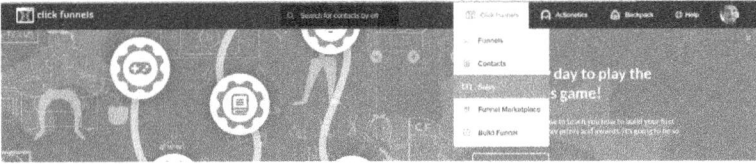

This will open a list of buyers in the last 30 days (you can select other periods in the dropdown at the top of the screen):

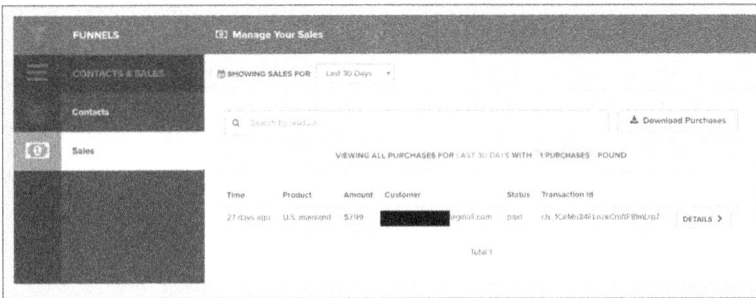

To access the customer's address, click on their email address in the Customer column. This will open up their individual record (I've blacked out the details in the picture .

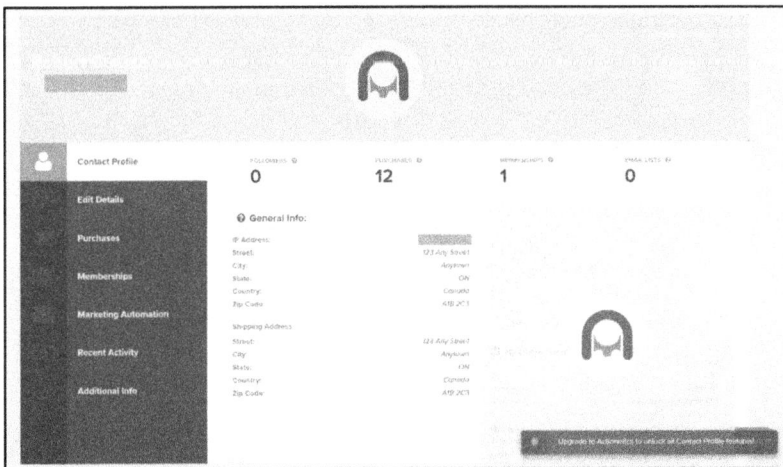

On this screen, you'll see two addresses. The one you need is the bottom one — the Shipping Address.

Other tabs on the left will tell you what products they have bought, what product memberships they currently have active, and what their recent activity has been (such as opting into your Reader Bonus funnel). The Marketing Automation tab is only active if you're using ClickFunnels' own automation platform, Backpack, which is part of their top tier subscription.

Moving on

We've completed the editing of the first page of your Free + Shipping funnel.

Remember to click [Save], then exit out of the editor to move to the next page.

25

Creating an Order Bump (Optional)

When I set up the shared funnel, I deliberately left the OTO turned off because I wanted to keep things as simple as possible. That said, I know that some readers of this book may want to set up a bump. So, if you're feeling comfortable with Click-Funnels and you feel ready to take on something extra, here's a quick guide to what you need to do.

If your OTO is going to be a digital product then things get trickier and it's beyond the scope of this book (though, as I wrote that, I decided what Volume 2 will be!) However, you actually have all the skills you need to create the order bump for a physical product.

What could that physical product be?

- Offer other books you've written on related topics
- Create an audio version of your book and put it on CD
- Create a video course of your book and put it on DVD
- Or, put those audio/video versions onto a USB stick instead of disks

- Create a workbook or journal of exercises that accompany the book
- Sell a physical product related to the topic of the book (e.g. if your book is about fitness, you could sell an item of exercise equipment).

Your OTO/Order bump is set up in almost the same way as the shipping charge.

1) The main (and obvious) difference is that you're going to check **Should This Product Be The Bump On The Order Page?**(!)
2) Set up a separate fulfilment email.
3) For email integration, you'll need to set up a new list and automation in ActiveCampaign.
4) In the automation, make sure you include a notification to you or an assistant to send out the bump product.

26

Page 2 – The first major upsell

Now that we've set up the sales page for your book offer, let's set up an upsell. Go back to the overview page for the funnel (if you're not there already) and click on the second page – OTO 1 Premium.

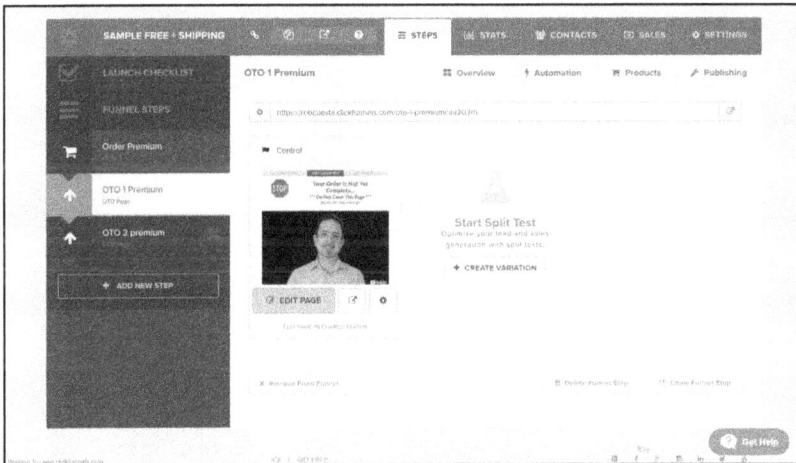

A note on OTO pages

OTO pages are a special kind of ClickFunnels page. The big difference between these and a standard Sales page is that they give you the ability to make a "one click upsell": the buyer won't have to enter their card details again as long as they don't close the page — if they buy the OTO product their card will be charged automatically.

Creating the OTO product

On this page, we're going to be offering the buyer the opportunity to invest even further with you.

Why not just put this as an order bump?

Well, if your upsell needs its own sales copy or sales video — or if the price is higher than an "impulse" buy — you can't put that into the order form, so you'll need to give the product its own sales page.

You'll need to create the product before you edit the page (you could do it without setting up the product, but it's easier if everything is set up in advance).

This is exactly the same as we saw in the previous chapter — *Setting up the shipping charge (and any OTO)* on page 209. Start the process by clicking the <PRODUCT> tab.

For now, you may want to make this a physical product — in a future book in this series I'll show you how to set up digital products in ClickFunnels.

Editing the page

Remember: you can change the name of the page by clicking on the <PUBLISHING> tab. After you've changed the name, scroll down to the bottom of the screen and hit [SAVE], otherwise your changes will be lost. Then click on <OVERVIEW> to get back to the page shown above and click the [EDIT PAGE] button.

Surprisingly, nothing in this page requires you to learn new skills.

The Progress Bar

The progress bar at the top is actually just a row with 3 columns. The middle column has been given a separate color, and the text in each row is simply a text box that you can edit.

The Video

This is a standard ClickFunnels video — edit it to add your own sales video for your product.

If you need help scripting a sales video, check out the demo of FunnelScripts; it also has a wizard for creating sales videos www.brightflamebooks.com/funnelscripts.

The Upsell

OTO pages support up to two products, but I'd only recommend you offer a single product on this page (and it's set up that way). If you want to offer a second, you can offer it on the next page.

Normally, I'm not a fan of yes/no choices — I prefer to give buyers a choice of what they want to buy rather than whether or not they want to buy. However, I appreciate that many readers of this book will already be thinking "What the heck am I going to sell them on this page?" So, making you come up with two offers would be cruel!

Finally, click save and come back to the overview page.

27

Page 3 – The second OTO

There's a third page to the funnel, which we'll be using to thank the reader for getting this far, tell them what's happening next, and potentially upsell them some more products or books!

> If you're going to want to upsell a product, make sure you set it up on the <PRODUCT> tab for this page before you click on [EDIT PAGE].

Editing the page content

Once again, there is nothing here that is new. You know how to edit the headlines, the texts, and the images. The buttons are ClickFunnels buttons, which you can edit exactly as we did on page 149 (*The Review Button*).

Adding an upsell

Currently, the page doesn't actually promote a product. However, if you look at Step #2, you'll see that it could easily be turned into a product sale.

After you've edited the headline and the text, edit the button settings. To make this a one-click upsell, click the button to edit its settings, and click the green [SET ACTION] button. Click on 1-CLICK UPSELL – CHOOSE PRODUCT and then pick your product from the dropdown that appears.

The product wall

At the bottom of the page, there's a row of buttons with images and text. Simply change the text and image for each button as usual.

You can use these to sell additional products or your other books, or to offer more free resources. These aren't one-click upsells: to buy, you'll be sending people to the sales page where you sell the product, the Amazon page for your book, or the lead capture page for your resources.

I also suggest you make these buttons open in a new window — keep the visitor on the OTO page as long as possible.

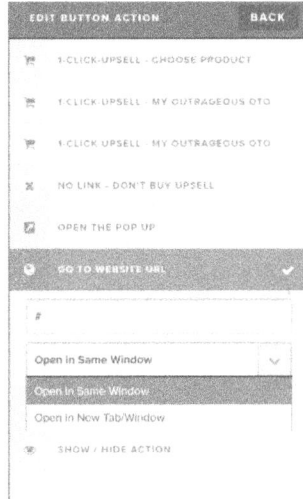

Moving on

Don't forget to set the SEO data (page title, etc.) in SETTINGS. For these inner pages, always set them to be invisible to search engines. Finally, click SAVE and exit.

For your funnels, you can make the front page visible to search engines, but you should always hide the later pages. You don't want someone finding your delivery pages without opting in!

28

A warning about the ClickFunnels plugin

If you use WordPress for your websites, I mentioned that there is a ClickFunnels plugin that allows you to create links to ClickFunnels pages that look like they are on your page.

DO NOT USE THE PLUGIN FOR THE FREE + SHIPPING FUNNEL.

I had a very frustrating two weeks the first time I set up a Free + Shipping funnel, where I was driving traffic and there were just NO orders coming in. Finally an equally frustrated customer emailed me to say she wanted top pay for the book, but every time she tried, the page was hanging.

The ClickFunnels plugin makes the page look like it's on your site — which, of course, is its big advantage. The problem is, when the transaction data is submitted to the payment company (in my case, Stripe) it detects the mismatch between where the transaction says it's coming from (your site), and where it's really coming from (ClickFunnels) and it gets flagged up as a potential fraud.

The answer is to use a redirect plugin that forwards the visitor to the ClickFunnels page but doesn't hide the ClickFunnels URL. On my own sites, I use one called Easy Redirect Manager.

Remember

Don't use the ClickFunnels plugin for order pages. Instead, use a redirect plugin that doesn't hide the destination URL.

29

The Burning Platform

The email sequence for your Free + Shipping offer is built primarily to create Scarcity, another of the psychological triggers Cialdini identified in *Influence*.

In the sequence, you're going to upsell a product but give the reader a deadline by which they have to buy, otherwise something negative—a price rise, the loss of a bonus, perhaps even not being allowed to buy at all.

Many experts are afraid of using scarcity. They think it's manipulative or too salesy. Let me put it into a different light.

Whenever I ask a business owner to name their biggest competitor, they usually have a long list of other businesses providing more or less similar solutions to their market. The more enlightened ones realize they are also in competition with any business that their customers could spend money with. Hardly anyone, however, lists the biggest deal killer of all.

Your biggest competitor—the one thing that will stop most of your potential customers buying—is *inertia*. Quite simply, given the choice, people would rather do nothing.

Usually, however, they try to fool you — and themselves — by saying that they "need to think about it" or they'll "review the details more carefully later" or some other excuse. The problem is, "later" all too often becomes "never" and the sale doesn't happen.

Now, think about this: when that happens, they're not getting the solution you could have provided to their problem. In other words, if you let people procrastinate and defer, *you are prolonging their pain needlessly*.

So, if you want people to buy, you need to give them a reason to buy now — what I call *the burning platform*: an action to take with a rapidly approaching deadline and a painful consequence for not acting by the deadline.

The problem is, creating real scarcity with a book is actually quite hard. By *real* I mean that the consequences of not taking action are strictly enforced: in other words, you warned them that the price would go up, and when they look the next day, the price really has gone up.

The reason, of course, is that you don't know, in most cases, when people are going to buy. So, you'd have to give each reader a personal deadline and be sending them to different versions of the sales/order page based on when they visit it.

But if you don't enforce the consequences — if the deadline passes and there is no loss — you've created false scarcity, which is a dangerous thing: you're training your list to understand that you don't mean it when you tell them they have to buy, and that they can wait as long as they like. The very first transaction with your new customer has just killed every other sale you would have made to them.

What will we make scarce?

So, how do we create scarcity for the upsell after someone orders your book?

The first decision you need to make is whether you are going to tie the scarcity to the product itself or to a bonus. It's the difference between "We only have ten of these at this price, so buy now!" and "The first ten buyers get this high-value bonus."

I don't like giving definitive opinions on "what works better" — you should always test your offers with your market — however, putting scarcity around bonuses has one major advantage: it is easy to swap one set of bonuses for another, and most people won't notice. You could, for example, decide that you're not going to offer a free consultation any more, but that you will instead run a free webinar. It's much harder to alter the main offer: it's painful to maintain multiple versions of a product, for example. As it happens, however, the ideas below apply equally whether you are creating scarcity around the main offer or the bonuses. Just remember to update your email sequence any time you change the offer, the bonuses, or the deadline.

Timed Launch

One way to create real scarcity is to have a fixed book launch period and force people to buy the book — and the upsells — during that period.

This forces all your buyers onto a fixed schedule that you control. The side benefit of this, of course, is that with everyone moving through at the same time, you can launch things like group programs on the back of it. And even if your upsell doesn't require people to all join at the same time, doing it this way is great for cashflow.

Don't assume, either, that "launch" means you can only do it once. You can have a launch as often as you want—just beware of teaching your tribe that they can wait because if they miss this launch another one will be along soon.

By the way, if you want to learn how to run a super-successful book launch, that's already planned as the topic of a future book.

Live Event

Another way to create real scarcity is to have a live event— or anything else with a fixed date—tied to the book and restrict the number of tickets. In this case, the deadline is not a fixed date but rather the threat of finding that all the tickets have been sold.

Again, you can do this more than once, but there's a risk that buyers will spot the pattern and tell themselves they can wait. You can avoid that by offering a discount on tickets only for the *next* event: if they wait for the one after, they'll have to pay full price.

Restricting Quantity

One of the most basic forms of scarcity is to simply say that you are only going to sell a fixed number of the upsell, and once it's gone it's gone.

You can reinforce this by having a countdown of the units remaining on your sales page. Since this number would have to be updated manually, I'll leave it up to your sense of honesty and fair play how often you update it and how accurate the count is!

Diary-Driven Scarcity

One very powerful form of scarcity that works very well in "expert adviser" industries is to upsell something that involves making an appointment.

For example, you could sell a product but offer a "free" consultation as a bonus (it's not really free because they've had to buy the product, so you've been paid). That allows you to include wording along the lines of "My diary fills up very quickly, and I'm only offering a small number of these session. If you order today, you can book a free consultation. But, if you contact me tomorrow, you may find that my diary is fully booked."

Changing the Offer

Making changes to the offer or the bonuses is a convenient way to force scarcity. It allows you to say honestly "This offer disappears on March 1st. After that date, it will be gone, and you won't be able to get this package anywhere."

Then, on 1st March, you change the bonuses and your integrity is maintained.

And you can do that as often as you like or need — say every three months — as long as you can keep coming up with new packages.

It has the added advantage that it keeps your offers fresh: rather than promoting the same package, year in year out, and boring your tribe, you can keep them engaged and guessing what the latest package will be.

30

The Soap Opera Sequence

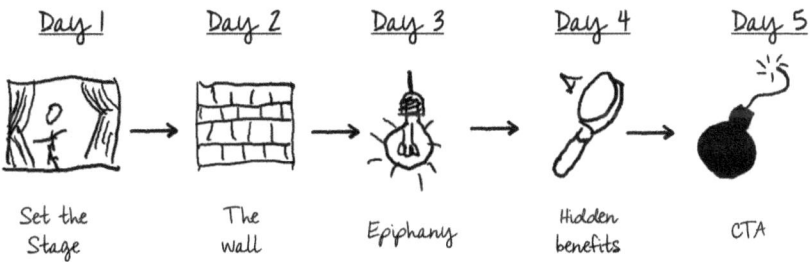

For our Free + Shipping funnel, we're going to create what's called a Soap Opera sequence.

The Soap-Opera Sequence

Day 1	Day 2	Day 3	Day 4	Day 5
Set the Stage	The Wall	Epiphany	Hidden benefits	CTA

If you want more detail about this type of email sequence, read Russell Brunson's book *Dotcom Secrets*.

You can get it free (just pay shipping!) at

http://brightflamebooks.com/dotcomsecrets

The soap opera sequence is a five-day email sequence.

1) In the first email you're going to be setting the stage: "This is what my life was like. And tomorrow let me tell you about the biggest challenge I had."
2) In the second you describe an obstacle that you faced at some point in your life (which is really about how you got into this business): "This is the biggest challenge I ever had. And tomorrow let me tell you how I got through it."
3) On day three you tell them about the epiphany you had that allowed you to get through that brick wall: "This is the realization I had, and tomorrow I'll tell you about some benefits that I hadn't expected."
4) On day four you tell them about the hidden benefits of solving the problem.
5) Day five is the call to action with a deadline: "Here's what you need to do, but it's going away soon, so act now."

> You can add the automation directly to your ActiveCampaign account using this link:
>
> **http://tplshare.com/fOXeRKu**

Just in case you're using a different autoresponder, here's the text of each of the emails, so you can see what they look like in practice.

> You can also download the text of all the emails by registering your copy of this book at
> **www.BrightFlameBooks.com/FunnelBonus**

Email 1: Setting the stage

SUBJECT: Thanks for ordering Premium

Hey %FIRST-NAME%,

We got your order for your free copy of {TITLE}, and my team is on the case. We'll ship it in a few days, but while you wait I wanted to welcome you "officially" into my world.

THEN YOU TELL A LITTLE STORY ABOUT HOW YOU GOT INTO THIS BUSINESS

About 15 years ago, I walked out of a well-paid job with one of the biggest management consulting firms in the world to pursue a crazy dream: starting my own business.

Like so many new entrepreneurs, I struggled for the first few years. I couldn't get enough clients, and when I did, I was afraid to charge what I was worth because I thought they wouldn't pay. It almost drove me bankrupt.

When I finally figured out how to make the business work, I made myself a promise: to share what I'd learned with other professionals--coaches, consultants, speakers and other people who make their living by selling what they know--so that they wouldn't have to go through the pain I suffered.

I also set myself a goal: to give away better stuff for FREE than many people charge for.

And tomorrow, I'll do exactly that: I'm going to give you {COMPELLING DESCRIPTION OF YOUR GIFT}... BUT only if you open the email when it arrives...

Yes, that's right. I want to make sure we get off to a great start.

You see, one of the things I teach my own clients is that when you give great value for free, the people who get the best results from it--the people it has the most impact on--will seek you out and hire you.

So it makes sense to give great value and not hold back.

Sounds good?

Great. Then make sure you watch out for that email tomorrow.

Thanks

{your name}

P.S. The subject line is {subject of day 2 email}-- so keep your eyes open!

Notice that final PS: it's a really clever way to increase your email open and read rates. We are all inundated with emails these days, and it's easy for emails to get ignored. Telling your readers to look out for a specific subject line gets them waiting for it and makes it much more likely that they'll notice it and actually open it.

Email 2: The wall

Subject: 2 of 5: My MBA never prepared me for this!

I stared at the screen in disbelief.

$300.

How the hell could ANYONE be making money selling a twelve-day live training course for that?

It was 18 months since I'd been certified as an NLP trainer, and things weren't going well. I was running the same business model as other NLP schools: a free half-day seminar, with a six-weekend training course as the upsell.

I'd started out at $1,000 per person for the course, but I wasn't getting enough people, so I dropped it to $800. Only, instead of getting more people, I got less!

And then one day, I was searching online and I found a competitor selling the same kind of course for $500. I'd have to get 15 people into the course just to break even at that price!

I'd known for a while that the market was bad: there were dozens of competitors just in London where I ran my courses. And we were all selling pretty much the same thing: the courses were all about the same length, and the content was basically identical.

The only differentiator was: price.

I thought about that $500 price point.

I remember burying my head in my hands and sobbing. I couldn't compete. At $500 per person I was going to go bust the next time I ran a course.

I knew that other NLP trainers were struggling too. Some of them had never even managed to make enough to recover the costs of certification. Costs they'd mostly put on credit cards, which meant they were carrying that debt, paying interest, and wondering if they'd ever be able to pay it off.

I knew I had to do something. I knew I couldn't compete with those people giving away their courses for $500.

So far, everything has been story — there's not a lot of "showing" initially. But, it's been leading up to this point, which is the tease to get them to read the next email.

And that was when I had an epiphany.

Would you like to know what it was? Are you interested in how I was able to transform my business, charge TEN times what my competitor was charging, and end up working with executives form some of the largest companies in the world and teaching NLP to ... well actually I can't tell

you that because if I did, a line of black cars would appear outside my door and I'd be whisked off to some place that doesn't appear on any maps... you get the picture.

Watch out for my email tomorrow, and I'll show you the realization I had.

So, look out for tomorrow's email: the title is {insert subject of email 3}

{NAME}

P.S. I almost forgot. Yesterday I promised that I was going to GIVE you {compelling pitch} for free...

You can get it here. Please don't share this link with anyone: it's only for members of the "family":

{LINK}

This {description} has helped more of my students to {big promise} than anything we've done in the past. So signup right now, and let's see what it does for you!

'Til tomorrow!

Note: A really good idea for the day 2 gift is to give them free access to a product for a limited time — say seven days — and only ask them to pay if they like it.

Email 3: The Epiphany

Subject: 3 of 5: my game, my rules

I was sitting with my pen and a calculator, and I couldn't make the numbers work.

If I charged $500 for my 12-day course, the way some of my competitors were, I couldn't deliver to the standard I wanted to. I'd be running it in a church hall or community center, and I still wouldn't be making any money, because of my hotel costs.

But if I tried to charge "the market rate", I knew I just couldn't get enough people through the door.

That's when I realized that I didn't want to compete with either of them!

If you've read the chapter "There's No Such Thing as Market Rates" in Premium, then you'll have seen my illustration of the competition curve. Competition is a bell curve: in any market, most seller end up charging something around an average price--the so-called "market rate". If you're on the wrong side of that bell curve, on the left, then the only way to reduce competition is to drop your prices to the point where other people just don't want to compete with you. That's what I'd been doing steadily over the previous 18 months.

If you try to raise your fees a little, you move closer to the center of the curve, where there's more competition, so you make even less money.

But think about it: why don't people want to compete at that lower end? Because they can't make any money. And if they can't, neither will you.

As I stared at the sheet of paper with my calculations, I doodled that curve, and I realized I didn't want to be at the lower end, and I didn't want to be in the middle either.

So I raised my prices.

In a market where most people were trying to sell at around $1200 and some idiots were struggling at $500, I went first to $1600 and finally to $3000.

Suddenly, I had merchant bankers signing up. Senior civil servants. People were flying in from overseas to attend. I had other training companies asking me to deliver my courses to their clients.

From struggling to break even, I had one of my most successful years ever.

And I did it by focusing on one thing: refusing to play the game my competitors were. I changed the game and changed the rules of competition.

Would you like to know how I did that? I just posted a video online that shows you how I {DE-

SCRIBE YOUR TRANSFORMATION} and turned
it into {DESCRIBE YOUR BIG RESULT}.

I posted the video here: {LINK TO YOUR FREE
BONUS}

Check it out and let me know your thoughts.

Thanks

{NAME}

P.S. Tomorrow I want to show you a few hidden
benefits that {your special sauce} will give you:
benefits you probably didn't even realize exist.
Watch for tomorrow's email!

Most of the content of this email is a retelling of part of the
book. Why? Because it's a strong story that will hopefully make
them want to read the book — and remember, they're still waiting for the print book to come in the mail, so it may even get
them to order the Kindle version, even though the paperback is
on its way!

For the free bonus in the email, you can use one of the videos
you give them as a bonus for reading the book. If you do that,
then the link can take them to your reader bonus funnel.

Email 4: Hidden Benefits

Subject: 4 of 5 – The hidden benefits

When I first started charging premium rates, I worried that I didn't have a big brand. I didn't have fancy offices, high-profile clients or anything.

I just knew that people who attended my courses were getting massive shifts, and I wanted to share it.

But what really rocked my raising my prices opened doors. Companies that would never have looked at me when I was charging $1000 suddenly wanted to talk to me. I started to get invited to speak at conferences. I was even runner-up in a national business contest.

I started working with global clients who flew me around the world. I was living a James Bond lifestyle and getting paid very nicely for it.

And, of course, eventually I started to teach other experts how to do the same thing in their business.

But the REAL hidden benefit has been the fulfilment I get when I see someone else's business (and as a result, their life) transformed. And that is really what this business is about for me.

And if you're in my tribe, then I'm guessing you probably feel the same when you create transformation for your clients. Am I warm?

If so, then you NEED to sign up for my {BONUS PRODUCT}. Normally, I'd sell it for $XXX, but I'm going to do two cool things to make this a nobrainer for you.

First, {COMPELLING REASON TO ACT 1}.

Second , {COMPELLING REASON TO ACT 2}.

Yes, you read that right. you get {summarize reasons to act}.

And if you don't like it for ANY reason, {take away the risk}.

How does that sound?

Cool. Go grab your access here:

{LINK}

Thanks

{NAME}

This email does three things.

First, it establishes a lot of social proof.

Second, it builds some rapport around wanting to transform my clients, and suggests that they're the same (who, after all, is going to say they don't want to help their clients be transformed?) and therefore they should buy the product. Now, that works for me because my clients are also in business. If you sell to consumers, you'll need to find a "double bind" of your own: a reason for buying that they can't deny without making themselves look bad in their own eyes!

Third, of course, it pitches the product and establishes that there are going to be penalties for not taking action.

What product should you pitch? Well, you could sell anything, but the sensible option would be whatever you sold as the OTO on the second page of the funnel. Most of your readers won't have bought it at that stage, but that just means "not now" rather than "not ever." So, you may pick up some more sales by pitching them the OTO again.

Email 5: The Call to Action

Subject: 5 of 5: this is going away

Hey ,

I've been talking about {UPSELL PRODUCT} this week, and how you can {COMPELLING REASON TO ACT}. But I'm going to {TAKE-AWAY} ...

{DEADLINE}

Yes, I'm sorry, but if you read this email after {DEADLINE}, it will be too late.

If you want to get {UPSELL PRODUCT} after that, you'll have to {PENALTY}.

But, if you want to take me up on my offer to {compelling reasons to act} then...

Go get your access ASAP at:

{LINK}

You have been warned! I don't want you emailing me tomorrow saying you didn't know :)

So, go get {OFFER} and I'll see you inside!

Thanks

{NAME}

For this email, you'll need to decide what the penalty is for not taking action to create the scarcity I discussed above.

Will they end up paying more?

Will they have to buy another product, because the only way to get this one is as a bonus?

Will they have to attend a live training because that's the only other time you sell it?

You can get very creative with these reasons for taking action now.

31

The End or the Beginning?

Congratulations! If you've made it this far, you have two of the core funnels set up and working. Every expert-author needs five fundamental funnels to support them in using their book to build their business:

1) A **Reader Bonus** funnel to capture the contact details of people who have *read* your book.
2) A **Free + Shipping** funnel to build a list of *buyers*.
3) A **Street Team** funnel to recruit other people to help you spread the word about your book.
4) A **Ticking Timebomb** funnel to create momentum and excitement, and — with any luck — turn your book into a bestseller.
5) An **evergreen webinar** funnel to drive *qualified* leads to your business (especially useful for selling high-ticket offers).

In this book, I've given you step-by-step instructions for building the first two. In future books, I'll give you my entire blueprint for making high-ticket sales with an evergreen webinar and my bestseller book launch system for selling thousands of copies of your book in a short period of time. Make sure to register your copy of this book to be told when those books are released.

In addition, you'll get the following bonuses as a thank you for being a reader of this book:

- Clickable import links for all the funnels and email automations in this book.
- Editable files of all the sample emails so you can tailor them to your business and/or import them into any email software you want.
- A PDF edition of this book that you can print out and make notes on.
- Free updates to future editions of the book.

32

Resources

Check out the following for more detail or supporting information.

Expert Secrets

In *Expert Secrets*, Russell Brunson sets out his model for creating an expert business, starting a movement, and positioning yourself as the leader of that movement. You can get a free copy at http://brightflamebooks.com/expertsecrets

Dotcom Secrets

Dotcom Secrets was Russell Brunson's earlier book in which he set out the fundamentals of selling online, whether you're selling information, product, or services. You can get a free copy at http://brightflamebooks.com/dotcomsecrets

108 Split Tests

This is one of my favorite reference books when I'm setting up websites and funnels—although the format is more like a giant magazine. It documents 108 tests that Russell Brunson and his clients carried out, changing colors, wording, even the positioning of elements on the page, and much more. Each of the 108 tweaks in the book may only improve conversion by a fraction of a percent, but those 108 fractions soon mount up!

Get it from **http://brightflamebooks.com/splittestbook**

Funnel Scripts

Not everyone is a great copywriter, not everyone wants to learn copywriting, and not everyone can afford to hire a professional copywriter. With FunnelScripts you answer a series of questions about your offer and it generates the copy for it. You'll need to tidy it up, but it will greatly accelerate your copywriting.

It has wizards for everything from face-to-face sales to webinars, PPC ads to sales videos, and much more. You can watch a demo at **www.brighflamebooks.com/funnelscripts**

Sixteen Ways to Grow Your Business with a Book

Sixteen Ways is a short guide I created that sets out how you can use your book to generate leads, close deals and make money. Get a free copy at **www.brighflamebooks.com/16ways**

33

Work with BrightFlame Books

We work with experts like you at three key stages to help you position yourself as the leader in your industry.

Ready to write a book?

If you're **thinking about writing a book** to boost your personal brand and grow your business, but you're not sure how to get started (or even what sort of book you should write), visit our main site at www.brightflamebooks.com to download free resources.

> If you think we'd be a good match, visit
> **www.brightflamebooks.com/getpublished**
> to fill out our brief questionnaire and request a consultation with me or one of our book coaches. We'll discuss your business and whether a book is the right next step for you.

Need help getting your book out into the world?

If you've written the first draft of your book and you need help to publish it and — potentially — to turn it into a bestseller, take a look at our launch support packages at

<u>www.brightflamebooks.com/yourbooklaunch</u>

Published a book but struggling to get clients with it?

If you've published a book but you're struggling to monetize it, visit <u>www.howexpertsgetclients.com</u> to find out about the Author-Expert Insiders Circle program. Insiders is designed for high-growth professionals who want to use their book to take their business to the next level.

This book is based on two modules of our Author-Expert Insiders Circle. Each month, Rob takes you step-by-step through implementing a strategy to use your book as a tool for getting leads, closing sales, and building your presence in the market.

You can find out more about joining the program at

<u>www.HowExpertsGetClients.com</u>
